"
… The vine may be very good, and the winemaker may be very good, but the resulting wine can be miserable, if Nature is not on man's side. "

Other Books Published by Maizal

Spanish	English	Bilingual
El Mate	The Mate	Teatro Colón
El Tango	The Tango	Pintura Argentina/
El Gaucho	The Gaucho	Argentine Painting
Argentina Natural	Argentine Nature	
La Cocina Argentina	Argentine Cookery	
Vinos Argentinos		

Acknowledgement,
María Daniela Riba D'Ave (revision), Martín Bomrad (photography), Santiago Aguirre Saravia (iconography), Francisco Weil (production), Florencia Alzugaray (photography).
Vinoteca La Vieja Damajuana (Santa Fe), Vinho e Coisas (Portugal), Oviedo (Nachtmann), APCOR (Portuguese Cork Association)
Alta Vista S.A., Altos las Hormigas S.A., Bodega Altos del Desierto, Bodega Augusto Pulenta, Bodega Benegas, Bodega Familia Zuccardi, Bodega Jean Rivier e Hijos, Bodega La Rosa, Bodega Michel Torino Cafayate, Bodega Navarro Correas, Bodega Norton, Bodega Ruggeri, Bodegas Chandon, Bodegas Etchart, Bodegas Hispano Argentinas, Bodegas Lagarde S.A., Bodegas Lavaque S.A., Bodegas López, Bodegas Nieto Senetiner, Bodegas Salentein, Bodegas Terrazas de los Andes, Bodegas Trapiche, Bodegas Valentín Bianchi, Bodegas y Cavas de Weinert S.A., Bodegas y Viñedos de Peñaflor, Bodegas y Viñedos Leoncio Arizu S.A., Cooperativa Quintana, Dolium S.A., Domain Vistalba S.A., Establecimiento Humberto Canale S.A., Finca Altamira, Finca Escorihuela Gascón, Finca Flichman S.A., Finca La Anita, Fincas Catena Zapata, La Rural Bodegas y Viñedos S.A., San Pedro de Yacochuya S.A., Viniterra.

Argentrip
Argentina's on-line travel guide
www.argentrip.com

© Raúl Riba D'Ave, 2002
Book and Cover Design: Christian le Comte and Sophie le Comte
Hecho el depósito que marca la ley 11.723
I.S.B.N. 987-9479-04-1, Buenos Aires, Argentina
Editado por Maizal
Muñiz 438, B1640FDB, Martínez
Buenos Aires, Argentina.
e-mail: lecomte@cvtci.com.ar
Impreso en octubre de 2002.
Impreso por Morgan Internacional.

Raul Riba D'Ave

Argentine Wines

MAIZAL
EDICIONES

Foreword

In literature we will find countless works and volumes that deal with wine. And, we wonder: why has this exquisite drink, obtained from the fermentation of grape juice, caught man from the beginning of time?

The ancients had already differentiated wine from all other alcoholic drinks such as beer for instance, giving it a value beyond man himself. This is precisely what makes wine so fascinating, because it has a cultural value; it is a fruit of civilisation.

Since Noah, wine has been the real partner of man; it has accompanied him in his moments of glory and in his moments of defeat. Among the many different types of drinks, only wine has acquired a sacramental and healing meaning. It was for centuries a universal antiseptic for most of the peoples. "When wine is missing, then drugs are necessary" is stated in the Old Testament. Wine was described as being a tonic for body and soul, an antidote to melancholy, fatigue and indigestion, and as a component of happiness and good humour. Today, modern medicine has discovered numerous attributes with which wine can benefit our health.

Wine adapts itself to a great variety of tastes. The way it is being cultivated, the climate, the terroir, the form of production, among other factors, contribute to make wine attractive for its diversity.
It also possesses other attributes, since its quality grows with time. This ageing implies complexity and harmony. So in the cup, vineyard, wine and man become one and they reflect the civilisation that has produced it.

It is because of this, that some time ago, when I received the manuscript of "Argentine Wines" by Raúl Riba D'Ave, I felt a double responsibility. I had not only to write about a fascinating and exciting subject, but I had also the honour of writing the prologue to this book that we are presenting now.

"Argentine Wines" not only explains the different features associated with wine and its production, but it presents the noble materials related to it and the culture that receives it.

The transparency of his writing, not only because of his style, but because of its contents as well, is admirable. Many people write about wine, but only a few write from the heart. This book contains the most important topics about the world of wine, treated in a synthetic way, didactic and pleasant, allowing the reader to have access to Argentine wines following its own history.

Vineyards and wines were the true witnesses of time, since the foundations of the cities in Cuyo were the economy grew, thanks to this wonderful drink.

In this book by Raúl Riba D'Ave, the Old and the New World of wine get together and bear the fruit of Argentine Wines.

Prof. Adriana Ruth de la Mota

The History of Wine in Argentina

It was only after the arrival of Christopher Columbus at the West Indies in 1492, that the "Vitis vinifera", the only variety of vine that generates appropriate grapes for wine production, started being grown in America.

According to the theories about the history of wine production in Argentina, the first vines were planted in what is today the Province of Santiago del Estero. Christian missionaries brought the plants from Mexico in the middle of the XVI century, because they could not celebrate mass without mass wine. From Santiago del Estero, the cultivated area extended towards the south. Around the year 1569 the first vines were planted in Mendoza and San Juan.

From then on, this region was going to be the most important and most famous wine-producing region in Argentina.

There had been earlier attempts to plant vines in the southern region of the American Continent but the problems connected with the transportation of vine shoots from Europe were difficult to solve. The vine shoots, cut in Europe in winter, dried off during the journey or they started shooting when the ship crossed the Equator and the climate changed. Since this problem remained unsolved, the settlers started sowing grape seeds, which is probably the explanation for the many Creole grape varieties that exist in Argentina today. When grape seeds are sown, the resulting plants will not reproduce the same characteristics as the original one.

See glossary on page 120.

Drinking wine was deeply rooted in the culture of all European settlers, especially those who arrived in America coming from Spain and Portugal. Wine was not only drunk to complete their Mediterranean diet but it was used to stimulate the recovery of sick people as well. Catholic missionaries also needed wine for their religious celebrations.

Vineyard, Bodegas Etchart

But, the large development of the production of wine in Argentina started much later. It was around the year 1883, and two important factors contributed to this expansion: the creation of the "Quinta Normal de Agricultura" in Mendoza, the first agriculture school in Argentina, and the inauguration of the railway line between Mendoza and Buenos Aires, in 1885.

John Miers "Wine production, elaboration of must", 1826

An additional factor helped this development at the turn of the century: the inrush of a large number of European immigrants who arrived in Argentina, particularly those who came from Spain and Italy, and then, some time later, also from France. They came from countries, which were traditionally wine producers and wine consumers. Nothing would have changed without the help and efforts of these immigrants; the wine production would have never developed in what it is today: Argentina is one of the largest wine producers in the world.

However, until recently, the wine produced in Argentina was, to a large extent, of a very common quality.

Production concentrated on satisfying the enormous demand of the domestic market, relegating quality to a secondary level.

Christiano Junior (1832-1883) "Agricultural School"

Quality wines represented only a small part of the total production, which was entirely devoted to the production of table wines. These common wines were sold indiscriminately in *damajuanas* (recipientes similar to a demijohn with about 5 liter capacity), usually with no label at all.

In the 70s, when the consumption of wine in Argentina reached its highest level: 90 litres per capita, drastic changes started happening.

The consumption of wine fell abruptly. Today only 38 litres of wine are drunk.

Barrel production of the famous "El Vasquito", Bodega de José López y Hnos, 1910.

Where there used to be a glass of wine, today we find a glass of beer. Due to an aggressive marketing, beer had arrived and conquered. The reason was not only the lower price, but beer seemed to better adapt itself to the way of life of the new generations, who had been seduced by this brilliant blonde of refreshing flavour.

Wine was then regarded as something belonging to the past.

There had to be a renovation and the change had to happen at product level. It was necessary to relegate quantity in favour of quality, which had been the method used by all other wine producing countries. The world market demanded quality wines and as all its competitors of the New World (United States, Australia, Chile, South Africa, New Zealand), Argentina was also capable of producing them.

The country began to take its first steps in its own quality wine producing revolution at the beginning of the 80s. In less than 10 years an important reduction of wine producing areas took place.

Disorganised or abandoned vineyards were eliminated, the less noble vines were uprooted and superior vines were orderly planted using better methods and separating the different varieties, especially those that were internationally considered as adapting themselves to the production of the best fine wines. The wineries invested in technology in order to achieve the quality of the wines of its competitors.

Bodegas Bianchi

It was then that many foreign wineries got interested in this "sleeping giant" that was Argentina's wine producing area and started investing in national wineries. They became aware of the existence of a large potential in this healthy land which adapted itself so wonderfully to vine cultivation, and which is, virtually, inexhaustible in extension.

This huge inflow of foreign capital and experience in the national wine-producing scene was extremely important in this process which has definitely not finished yet.

Saint Felicien Prize Fine Arts Museum Label by Clorindo Testa

Today in Argentina, wine culture is generating a growing interest in the consumer and this is due to the great increase in quality of national wines and the marketing associated with it.

The consumer is no longer interested in common wine or the wine in damajuanas, he is looking for bottles with prestigious labels and wines that create pleasant sensations.

Nicolás Rubió "Trampling the Grapes", 2002

Wine is regarded today as a noble beverage, a symbol of good taste, the link between men and the joie de vivre. Not only in Argentina, but the entire world over.

Argentine Wine in the World

*Massen's Winery,
Mendoza,
XIX th Century*

TERRA

*Terra
Cabernet/Syrah
Vintage 1997
Casa Vinícola
Viniterra*

The Argentine wine-producing segment has today an important place in the world.

According to the last world statistics of the O.I.V. (International Office of Vineyards and Wine) Argentina is the fifth wine producer in the world, after France, Italy, Spain and the United States and the sixth according to per capita consumption.

Argentine wine started having a better presence outside its boundaries after 1995. Exports in 1995 were exceptionally high due to reasons beyond national control: there was a shortage in the production of the most important wine-producing countries in Europe caused by frost and droughts.

However, since then, the growth of the participation of Argentine products in the world market presented itself as stable with a long-term tendency.

What was really auspicious for Argentina was that from then on, it was included among the countries with a growing wine producing industry.

Yet, it is still not easy to find Argentine wine in the rows of shelves at supermarkets or wine shops abroad.

In the United Kingdom, one of the most important wine markets in the world, Argentine bottles are scarce. Compared with the other countries of the New World of wine, Argentina has less presence in the market. This is not for historic reasons, because in the United States, an equally important market of reference, Argentina has a similar status as her main competitors.

Although today more and much better wines are exported than ten years ago (especially if value is compared), there is still a long way to go. Argentina will have to seduce international palates with the

Bodega Catena Zapata, Fincas Catena Zapata

new wines it is producing. One has to bear in mind, that Argentina started its "wine revolution" much later than the other countries, so the results will arrive later too.

Adopting this philosophy, that just quality counts (without forgetting its relation with the price) and launching innovative products accompanied by an intelligent marketing, Argentine wines will continue growing in prestige in the world market and they will start conquering consumers who nowadays buy wines from other countries.

Cadus, Malbec Bodegas Nieto Senetiner

The consumer today looks for a bottle that contains romance and treasures, all those good and new sensations that he wants to discover and appreciate, to be able to recommend them to his friends.

This is the secret of a good wine and a good wine will have, sooner or later, a guaranteed success.

Varietal Wines versus Blended Wines

Finca Flichman Dedicado 1997 The Finca Flichman Dedicado 1996 won the Civart Price in 1999 in Bordeaux

Alamos Chardonnay Recently the Catena Zapata Winery launched its varietal wines Alamos with a very good relation price/quality into the domestic market. The Chardonnay Alamos 2000 was granted the Gold Medal at the International Wine Challenge 2002-UK and the "Chardonnay Trophy".

Each grape variety has its unique characteristics as regards form, colour of the berry, leaves, clusters, etc. Due to these characteristics, each grape variety generates a wine of its own, identifiable because of its aroma and because of its flavour.

Wines made of only one variety of grapes, are called varietals (or monovarietals) and the label carries the name of the grape variety used.

The Argentine law regulates that these wines cannot be made with less than 80% of the grape variety stated on the label. In Europe this percentage is 85% and in the United States a more generous law allows a varietal wine to be made with only 75% of the referred grape variety.

If wine is produced with 100% of the same variety, then it is called "pure varietal". Today it is common to find an accurate explanation of the composition of the wine on the counter label of the bottle.

Varietals are a recent trend, something that appeared in the 70s, launched by the winemakers in the United States as an alternative to European wines that were produced in specific regions. The type of grape variety is contrasted with the characteristics of a given region, with a specific soil and climate. Wines made of the same grape variety can be produced in different areas in the world.

The reason for the emergence of wines called "varietals" in the New World is particularly associated with the absence of classification of defined regions and the corresponding denominations of origin as in Europe. New World wine makers needed a simple classification in order to name the style of the wine.

There existed an old legal problem between the two continents (Europe and America) because the new continent constantly used the names of European denominations of origin to classify the wines according to their style.

Cellar,
Bodegas Etchart

The use of the name of the grape in order to define a wine was the simplest way to overcome this problem. The name of the grape variety was not protected as the denominations of origin were. It proved to be technically easier to call the wines according to the grape varieties used than to establish a totally new system of defined and controlled wine producing regions. On the other hand, this new way of production and classification had a very important advantage, which the producers had not realised at the very beginning.

Dolium
Malbec Reserva
Varietal wine
Dolium

*Don Valentín
Lacrado
Blended red wine
Bodegas Bianchi*

*Vineyards,
Bodegas Etchart*

*Don Nicanor
Blended red wine
Bodegas
Nieto Senetiner*

*Iscay
Blended red wine
Malbec and Merlot
Bodegas Trapiche*

The American consumer, not so well accustomed to the complicated denominations of European wines, preferred this new system because it was easier to associate the grape variety with the particular style of the wine.

It was much simpler to say that a wine was a Chardonnay and another a Merlot. The wineries, in spite of having different wine brands, produced at least types of wine that the consumer could identify within the styles he was familiar with.

The truth is that this trend of varietal wines, be it for its simplicity or for its novelty, expanded all over the world, including Europe.

However, the best wines in the world continue to be blended wines, which are the wines produced with two or more types of grapes. This does not mean that there are not any excellent varietal wines. There are. But to give the winemaker the possibility of mixing different types of grapes in the production of wine is giving him the opportunity to play with the unique characteristics of each grape variety and develop a well-balanced product.

There are grape varieties that have a better colour intensity, others contribute to a better structure, still others generate a more delicate wine, etc. If this true art is well managed, one gets a glorious result.

If we gain balance and harmony with a blended wine, with a varietal wine we have the possibility of appreciating the characteristics of a single grape, because the taste is totally isolated, especially in the pure varietals.

In Argentina, the trend to produce varietals started later than in the rest of the New World of wine. Winemakers were accustomed to blend wines, they not only mixed several grape varieties but they used to blend different vintages as well because they tried to produce the same style of wine year after year.

In this extreme south of the American continent, it was quite common to name wines using European denominations of origin. Today this abusive use is still practised because according to the treaties signed with Europe, there is still a time of transition to abandon its use.

Names such as "Borgoña" (Burgundy), "Chablis", "Champagne", "Beaujolais", "Oporto" (Port) or "Jerez" (Sherry) are still used on the labels of Argentine wines to point out to the consumer what type of wine he is buying. Obviously, an Argentine "Burgundy" is totally different from a French "Burgundy". At the beginning, this was an indicator of the type of wine. Neither the soil nor the climate or the grape varieties were the same. It was very difficult then, that these wines could bear any resemblance to the original French wine. I do not want to say that Argentine "Burgundy" is better or worse. It is different. And fortunately so, because one of the best qualities of wines is its enormous diversity.

*Benegas Blend
Produced with Cabernet Sauvignon, Merlot, and Cabernet
Franc grapes
Bodega Benegas*

*Henry Gran Guarda
1997
Blended red wine
Bodegas Lagarde*

*Achával Ferrer
Quimera
Blended red wine
Finca Altamira*

Grape Varieties in Argentina

Apart from the Criolla varieties, which were probably the result of the vines sown directly from seeds, there are in Argentina a large number of grape varieties that were brought from Europe. Some of these grape

*Vineyard,
Viñedos y Bodega
La Agrícola (Bodega
Familia Zuccardi)*

INTA
*Mendoza Station
The identification of
all existent grape va-
rieties in Argentina
would have never
been possible without
the meticulous studies
of the National Insti-
tute of Agricultural
Technology, Mendoza
Station, between the
years 1940 and 1980.
However, there are
still some vineyards
where the existing va-
rieties have not been
correctly classified so
far, in spite of the
efforts undertaken in
the census carried
out in the year 1990.*

varieties were given incorrect European names due to faulty ampelography knowledge of the original European varieties. There is even a minority of these grape varieties that do have a known European name but are not the same grape as in its European homeland. Where the Criolla grape varieties are concerned, the predominant ones are the basic Criolla Grande (Big Criolla), Criolla Chica (Small Criolla), Uva Cereza (Cherry Grape) and Moscatel Rosado (Pink Moscatel). These staple grapes, which are largely grown in the country, do not yield grapes fit for a fine wine. They end up in common table wines or are used to prepare grape juice. In order to produce good, fine wines, more complex and better quality "vitis vinifera" varieties have been planted.

Predominant Red Grape Varieties in Argentina

Cabernet Sauvignon ✲ If there is a grape that adapted itself to the regions of the New World wherever it was planted, then that is the Cabernet grape. It is very resistant against illnesses and what is even more important; it produces wines of very high quality. Nevertheless it is a very aggressive variety because of its high content of tannin. This is the reason why the wines produced with a high percentage of this grape variety are wines that should be stored, wines that will need a certain time in the bottle to tame its astringency and roughness.

One of the best Argentine Cabernet Sauvignon that can be consumed now is the Catena Zapata Cabernet Sauvignon 1997 not only because its intrinsic quality but also because of the time it has spent maturing in oak barrels and then in the bottle to refine its tannins. Other good examples, but of a better relationship price/quality are the excellent Terrazas Reserva Cabernet Sauvignon 1999; Terrazas Gran Guarda; the Salentein Cabernet Sauvignon 1999 (and 2000); the Familia Castelani Beltrán Cabernet Sauvignon 1997 and 1999 and the Luigi Bosca Cabernet Sauvignon 1999. These wines can be consumed now, but they will improve if they are left 2 or 3 years to develop in the bottle. The wines made of this grape variety have an immense capacity of ageing.

Only patience is needed to be able to resist the temptation to drink them when they are still too young.

Luigi Bosca
Cabernet Sauvignon
Bodegas y Viñedos
Leoncio Arizu

Terrazas Reserva
Cabernet Sauvignon
Bodegas Chandon

Salentein
Cabernet Sauvignon
Bodegas Salentein

Cabernet Sauvignon
blooming,
Bodega Norton

Viniterra
Merlot
Viniterra

Humberto Canale
Merlot
Establecimiento
Humberto Canale

Salentein
Merlot
Bodegas Salentein

Merlot ⚜ In Argentina the production of this variety is still making its first steps. It is not easy to produce good wine from this grape since it can generate diluted wines if it is not grown in the suitable climate and soil. Nevertheless some Argentine winemakers such as Humberto Canale in Río Negro and Salentein or Ruggeri in Mendoza have already proved that they are making good progress producing excellent wines of this grape variety. For the time being there are just a few wines made of Merlot grapes. But, since the fascination for red wine varieties apart from Cabernet Sauvignon, grows in the market, the wineries continue investing in this variety without having so far reached the quality of the wines produced in the homeland of this grape. In the last three years, winemakers have increased the surface of Merlot vineyards because of the high demand of a public influenced by a trend coming from the North (USA), from the United States, where the Merlot wine is one of the preferred varieties.

The Merlot variety is playing an important role in blended wines. It is often mixed with a high percentage of Cabernet Sauvignon in order to soften the resulting product.

The best Argentine wines with Merlot grape are the Iscay from Trapiche (50% Malbec, 50% Merlot), and the Achával Ferrer 1999 (50% Malbec; 50% Merlot), which is very difficult to get because it was not produced in large quantities. As a pure varietal, we recommend the Humberto Canale Reserva Merlot 1998; the Salentein Merlot 2000 or the excellent, but difficult to find, Ruggeri Merlot 2000 Prestigio Roble.

Picking grapes by hand, Viñedos y Bodega La Agrícola (Bodega Familia Zuccardi)

Caballero de la Cepa Syrah Finca Flichman

Syrah ✳ This grape variety, characteristic of the Valley of the Rhône River in France, generates spicy wines in its place of origin, that can be stored for a long time, especially those from the region of Hermitage. In Australia, where it is known as Shiraz, it is also considered a high quality grape variety. Here in Argentina it generates fleshy and strong wines, not as spicy as the Shiraz wines from Australia, and much less than the French ones, but whith the same ageing potential.

Trapiche Syrah Bodegas Trapiche

The Syrah wine in Argentina is different. In spite of being quite a new varietal wine in this country, there is a growing interest for it and the sales do not stop growing. For those who are looking for the real essence of the Argentine Syrah, which is different from the Syrah from other countries, we recommend: Finca Flichman Caballero de la Cepa Syrah 1999; Trapiche Syrah 1998; Escorihuela Gascón Syrah 1999; Nieto Senetiner, Syrah 1999. From the small winery Ruggeri, we recommend the Ruggeri Syrah 2000 and the Ruggeri Syrah 2000 Prestigio Roble.

Escorihuela Gascón Syrah Finca Escorihuela Gascón

Nieto Senetiner Syrah Bodegas Nieto Senetiner

Malbec ꞏ This grape variety (also called Cot in France) is emblematic of Argentina where it has developed its best characteristics. Not even Cahors, its mother land, in the South of France, produces so exciting wines as those made in Argentina, especially in Luján de Cuyo and Tupungato (both in the Province of Mendoza).

Dolium
Malbec
Dolium

Alta Vista
Malbec Premium
Alta Vista

Angélica Zapata
Malbec Alta
Fincas Catena Zapata

San Pedro de Yacochuya
Malbec
San Pedro de Yacochuya

To taste its personality, we recommend those produced with a 100% of the Malbec grape variety and no oak, so that the exuberant aroma of these wines can be fully appreciated. If a more complex Malbec varietal wine is preferred, then some oak ageing is advisable.

Some good examples of both types that can be bought in Argentina are: Fabre Montmayou Malbec 1997; Escorihuela Gascón Malbec 1999; Cadus Malbec 1999 elaborated by the Bodega Nieto Senetiner; Finca La Anita Malbec 1997; Alta Vista Malbec Reserva 1999; Terrazas Reserva Malbec 1999; Terrazas Gran Guarda; Dolium Malbec 2000; Yacochuya Malbec 1999; Altos las Hormigas Reserva 2000; Angélica Zapata Malbec Alta 1995; Weinert Cosecha Especial 1977.

Escorihuela Gascón
Malbec
Finca Escorihuela
Gascón

A little more difficult to find are the Luca Malbec 1999 and the Susana Balbo Malbec 1999 (and 2000); Familia Castelani Beltrán Malbec 1999; Achával Ferrer Malbec 1999 (expensive and very difficult to find).

Espalier of Malbec vines, Bodegas Etchart

Because of its different style and the delicate touches in its evolution, do not miss Casona López Malbec 1996 which, before leaving for the market, aged in 5.000 litre oak casks from Nancy.

Achával Ferrer Malbec Finca Altamira

Finca La Anita Malbec Finca La Anita

Fabre Montmayou Malbec Domaine Vistalba

Terrazas Reserva Malbec Bodegas Chandon

Cadus, Malbec Bodegas Nieto Senetiner

Weinert, Malbec Bodega y Cavas de Weinert

Malbec Estrella Malbec Bodega y Cavas de Weinert

Altos Las Hormigas Malbec Viña Hormigas

Casona López Malbec Bodegas López

*Marqués de Griñon
Tempranillo Roble
Bodegas Hispano
Argentina*

*Finca el Portillo
Tempranillo
Bodegas Salentein*

*"Q", Tempranillo
Viñedos y Bodega
La Agrícola (Bodega
Familia Zuccardi)*

*Full Bins,
Viñedos y Bodega
La Agrícola (Bodega
Familia Zuccardi)*

Tempranillo ※ The Tempranillo grape variety also called Tempranilla, is surely, as the Malbec, the grape variety with more potential of development in Argentina. The quality of wines produced with this grape are up to the standards of its European relatives, those from Ribera del Duero, Rioja or Penedés in Spain, or from Douro and Alentejo, in Portugal (where it is called Tinta Roriz or Aragonês). The most important characteristics of an Argentine Tempranillo can be found even in not expensive wines. We can recommend the Marqués de Griñón Tempranillo 1997; the Tempranillo 1999 from Colección Adunka, or the Finca El Portillo Tempranillo 2000 (Bodega Salentein).

For those who want to taste something really outstanding, but in another price range, they have to look for the "Q" Tempranillo 1997 from Bodega La Agrícola, worthy of the many international prizes it has been awarded. The "Q" 1999 is also excellent.

Pinot Noir ≈ Pinot Noir is the grape variety used for the big wines of the Burgundy region, in France. It is also used for the production of champagne, giving it body and structure. In Argentina it is not widely grown because of its difficulty to adapt itself to a terrain and climate it is not accustomed to. Nevertheless, there are certain wineries that have reached good results with this delicate grape. One of them is the Bodega Salentein with its Primus Pinot Noir 1999.

Also Bodega La Agrícola has produced its Santa Julia Pinot Noir Innovación 2000, which has an unbeatable value for money. The Saint Felicien Estiba SF Pinot Noir 1996 or 1997 from Bodegas Esmeralda and the Marcus Gran Reserva Pinot Noir 2000 from Bodegas Humberto Canale are also worthwhile tasting. In some of these wines it is possible to identify the taste of soil and mushrooms, a very common characteristic of the Argentine Pinot Noir.

Marcus, Gran Reserva Pinot Noir Bodegas Humberto Canale

Primus Pinot Noir Bodegas Salentein

Sangiovese ≈ This grape variety of Italian origin is responsible for the big wines of Tuscany (Italy), as the Chianti or the Brunello di Montalcino. In Argentina, this variety is used in the production of young and soft wines, with an intense red colour and fruity taste. If it is not blended with another more heavy body grape variety, the resulting wine has to be drunk between 1 and 2 years after having been bottled so that the characteristics that make it famous, can be fully enjoyed. It is difficult to find Sangiovese varietals in the Argentine market because practically all of them are exported.

Santa Julia Innovación Reserva Pinot Noir, Viñedos y Bodega La Agrícola (Bodega Familia Zuccardi)

Benegas, Sangiovese Bodega Benegas

Bonarda * Most of the Bonarda raised in Argentina is an Italian grape called Bonarda Piamontese. However, there are some specialist that state that the Argentine Bonarda variety is not related to the Italian Bonarda variety, but to a grape variety called Corbeau.

Since Bonarda is the most widely grown variety in Argentina, it would be very difficult for winemakers to change its name. Probably due to its high yield, there were so many vineyards planted with Bonarda. Nowadays it is used in blends with other grapes, as for instance Malbec to produce the wines called "borgoña" in the domestic market.

The Bonarda variety is rarely used on its own for varietal wines, but there is a Bonarda (blended only with Sangiovese) from Bodega La Agrícola that impressed the jury at the International Wine Challenge, in England. The Santa Julia Bonarda-Sangiovese Roble 1998 won the gold medal, leaving without arguments those who thought that the Argentine Bonarda was a mediocre variety and that could only be used in the production of common wines. The Valbona Bonarda 1999 Roble from Bodega Augusto Pulenta, the Bonarda from Bodegas Nieto Senentiner, and the Finca El Retiro, Bonarda 1999 are also wines produced with this variety.

*Santa Julia
Bonarda-Sangiovese
Viñedos y Bodega
La Agrícola (Bodega
Familia Zuccardi)*

*Alamos
Bonarda
Fincas Catena Zapata*

*Valbona, Bonarda,
Crianza en Roble
Bodega Augusto
Pulenta*

*Josefa Díaz y
Clucellas (1852-
1917) "Fruit"*

*G. Mendilahrzu
(1857-1894)
"Self-portrait"*

*Finca El Retiro
Bonarda
Finca El Retiro*

Predominant White Grape Varieties in Argentina

*Primus
Chardonnay
Bodegas Salentein*

*Saint Felicien
Chardonnay Roble
Fincas Catena Zapata*

*Famiglia Bianchi
Chardonnay
Bodegas Valentín
Bianchi*

*Benegas
Chardonnay
Bodega Benegas*

Chardonnay ▪ This is the most widely used grape variety for the production of fine varietals in Argentina. In the world, the Chardonnay grape is considered "the king of white grapes", in Argentina it is also considered the king, but, probably in the future, this grape variety will have to share the throne with other noble grapes such as the Semillón, the Viognier or the Tocai Friulano. These grape varieties are now surprising Argentine consumers with the fantastic wines they are producing.

The Argentine Chardonnay is produced following the tendencies used in other New World wine producing countries, such as the United States or Australia.

The best examples are fermented and matured in small barrels of new oak. However, some wineries are starting to keep part of the wine in stainless steel tanks so that the taste of oak is not so persistent. The wine kept in tanks is afterwards blended with the wine developed in barrels.

This is how a structured wine is obtained, a wine with plenty of body but also with the characteristic aroma of fruit that this variety usually has: pineapple, mango, melon, lemon...

Wines that are fermented and developed in oak barrels taste of vanilla and butter and they leave a certain characteristic stickiness in the mouth.

There is probably no other white grape in the world, capable of originating such well-structured wines as the Chardonnay.

The best Argentine Chardonnay wines are produced in the high areas of Tupungato and Agrelo in the Province of Mendoza.

Alta Vista
Chardonnay
Premium
Alta Vista

Harvester,
Viñedos y Bodega
La Agrícola (Bodega
Familia Zuccardi)

This grape variety is extremely important for the definition of the character of a champagne or sparkling wine, because it gives the champagne harmony and balance. Many wineries produce this type of wine and several methods are used. The general tendency is still to ferment and develop them in oak barrels.

Since there are so many different brands, we are going to mention those that will give the consumer the best value. That is the case of the Chardonnay from Finca La Escondida, produced in the Province of San Juan. Since San Juan has a warmer climate and lower rainfall than Mendoza, it generates different wines with a solid aromatic personality.

"Q" Chardonnay
Viñedos y Bodega
La Agrícola (Bodega
Familia Zuccardi)

They are very interesting for those passionate wine lovers who are looking for new sensations; from Mendoza we can mention the Saint Felicien Chardonnay Roble 1999, the Alta Vista Chardonnay 2001, the Benegas Chardonnay 2000, and, in another price level, the excellent "Q" Chardonnay 1999 from Bodega La Agrícola and the Primus Chardonnay 1999 from Bodegas Salentein.

Serie Reservada
Finca La Escondida
Chardonnay
Finca La Escondida

Sauvignon Blanc ≈ Nowadays, to speak of Sauvignon Blanc is to speak of New Zealand, although, this grape variety originated in France.

The white wine from New Zealand produced with this variety gained such fame in the world for its quality that the grape started being interpreted as the emblematic grape of New Zealand, as the Malbec is the emblematic variety of Argentina.

In the Argentine market, there are many varietal wines made of the Sauvignon Blanc variety since there are many wineries producing it with the yield of the more than 700 hectares planted with it.

However, in Argentina, the Sauvignon Blanc is still generating wines not altogether original. They are well-balanced wines, capable to giving pleasure but with not enough appeal to make the Argentine consumer change his current choice for Chardonnay wines in what varietal white wines are concerned. Apart from this, the Sauvignon Blanc compared to the Chardonnay is less prone to bottle ageing because it oxidizes quickly.

Norton
Sauvignon Blanc
Bodega Norton

Rutini
Sauvignon Blanc
La Rural Bodegas y
Viñedos

Viñedos y Bodega
La Agrícola (Bodega
Familia Zuccardi)

Generally they are wines to be consumed within the year in which they have been bottled. The profile of these wines is very similar from winery to winery, probably because of a good clonal purity. The majority of the Sauvignon Blanc grapes that exist in Argentina have probably been grafted with the same

Watering system, Finca La Anita

clone of this grape variety. Argentine Sauvignon Blancs are easy to drink, but somewhat different to the Sauvignon wines from other countries. The Argentine examples can be identified by a less intense grapefruit aroma and by a peach skin or new-mown grass aroma. Sometimes, these wines also have a toast aroma that can be confused with the aroma of some oak matured Chardonnay wines. In the case of the Sauvignon Blanc this toast aroma comes exclusively from the grape or derivates from its fermentation, not from the oak, unless it has spent some time in oak barrels, which is rare in the examples of Argentina. Sauvignon wines also have a livelier aroma and taste due to their manifest natural acidity. The Sauvignon Blanc wines in Argentina offer an interesting alternative to those a bit "worn-out" Chardonnay wines and apart from that, they also offer a better relation price/quality with a wide range of brands available in the market. We recommend the following wines, all of them with a very good relation price/quality: Humberto Canale Sauvignon Blanc 2000; Norton Sauvignon Blanc 2000 (and 2001); Finca El Portillo (Bodega Salentein) Sauvignon Blanc 2000 (and 2001); Rutini Sauvignon Blanc 2001.

Humberto Canale Sauvignon Blanc Establecimiento Humberto Canale

Finca El Portillo Sauvignon Blanc Bodegas Salentein

*Lagarde Semillón
Cosecha 1942
Semillón
Lagarde*

*Humberto Canale
Semillón
Establecimiento
Humberto Canale*

*Finca La Anita
Semillón
Finca La Anita*

Semillón ∗ As the Sauvignon Blanc, the Semillón is a grape variety that adapts itself to the area of the Province of Río Negro. However, in Mendoza this grape variety can also generate very good wines, especially those coming from Tupungato (Valle de Uco) where this *terroir* compensates the normal lack of acidity that the Semillón may present in other areas of the Province of Mendoza. The real difference lies in that in the colder regions of the Province of Río Negro, the resultant wines show a strong mineral character and a superior acidity.

This French grape is quite versatile in its native country, participating in the blend of numerous common, white wines, but also in the blend of some high quality wines, as it is the case of the sweet white wines of the Sauternes region or of the best white wines from Bordeaux.

In Argentina it is one of the white varieties that can compete with the Chardonnay as regards its bottle ageing capacity.

Apart from the mythical Lagarde Semillón 1942 which is, due to its price, not accessible to ordinary mortals, there are some interesting wines made of this grape which are available in the market. Taste those produced by Humberto Canale winery in the Province of Río Negro or those from Finca La Anita in the Province of Mendoza. One interesting thing to do is to buy some bottles and from time to time taste one and see how the wine is developing in the bottle.

Cándido López (1840-1902) "Still Life" (detail)

Escorihuela Gascón Viognier Finca Escorihuela Gascón

Viognier • This white grape variety can be considered a novelty, not only in Argentina, but also in other countries including France, its native country, where it was almost extinguished in the past.

In the 90s an increasing interest became evident because of the big potentialities of this grape. In Argentina it is starting its ascent now but there are some wineries that have already produced good wines with this grape. The wines generated with Viognier in Argentina are, as in the rest of the world, very aromatic. It is not a grape variety easy to tame and one will have to wait to see the results of the wineries in the future.

You will be positively surprised by the already existing wines especially the Santa Julia Viognier Innovacion 2000; the Lagarde Viognier 2000 or the Escorihuela Gascón Viognier 2000 and the Bykos Viognier 2001 by Viniterra.

Lagarde Viognier Bodegas Lagarde

Santa Julia Innovación Reserva Viognier Viñedos y Bodega La Agrícola (Bodega Familia Zuccardi)

Finca La Anita
Tocai Friulano
Finca La Anita

Tocai Friulano ▪ There is absolutely no doubt that this grape variety is not related to the famous Tokay (or Tokaji) wines from Hungary, or the Tokay-Pinot Gris grape variety grown in Alsace (France). It has to be repeated again and again because there is a tendency to confuse them, especially because this is not a well-known grape variety in Argentina, or even in the world.

The Tocai Fruilano is a white variety that originated in Italy. In Argentina it generates very pleasant wines, with a firm personality. Those who want to experience a different and elegant white wine should try one produced with Tocai Friulano.

A good example is the Tocai Friulano from Bodega Jean Rivier of San Rafael in the Province of Mendoza; if it is possible, vintage 97, one of the best in the decade. Another example is the Finca La Anita Tocai Friulano 1999, an unoaked example, exclusively produced in stainless steel tanks. These are wines for those who are tired of the same aromas that most well-spred varieties of white wines usually have.

Jean Rivier
Tocai Friulano
Bodega Jean Rivier
e Hijos

Fernando Paillet (1880-1967) "Lunch at an Estancia"

Vineyards, Bodegas Salentein

Torrontés ✳ One has to distinguish three different types of the Torrontés grape variety: the Torrontés Mendocino, the Torrontés Sanjuanino and the Torrontés Riojano, which is the original Torrontés grape variety and the only one that should be allowed to be called Torrontés.

*Etchart Cafayate
Línea Internacional
Torrontés
Bodegas Etchart de
Cusenier*

Nevertheless, currently that is not what occurs and the other two varieties that bear the name Torrontés benefit from the fame of the Torrontés Riojano not having the same characteristics. To make things harder to undestand, the three Torrontés varieties are called by the names of these specific regions, what makes people believe that they come from those regions, but this is a mistake.

Indeed both the Torrontés Mendocino and the Torrontés Sanjuanino can be called by other completely different names, depending on the area where they are grown.

One has to bear in mind, that the only variety that should bear the name Torrontés is the Torrontés Riojano, which is grown in different regions of the country, not only in La Rioja, as the name denotes.

So, whenever one mentions the Torrontés, one is speaking of the Torrontés Riojano.

*San Pedro de
Yacochuya
Torrontés
San Pedro de
Yacochuya*

The real origin of this grape variety is even more curious because so far nobody has been able to establish where this variety really came from. It is not a Criolla variety and it has not been identified to be an European variety. It is believed that a Moscatel kind of grape (which the Torrontés bears a resemblance to) was crossed with a Criolla grape variety. This is why we may say that the Torrontés is probably exclusive of Argentina. The theory has not been confirmed and it is being studied at the moment to see if it belongs to a clone of any known European variety.

The truth is that the wines generated with this grape started been accepted in the international market, following the steps of the Malbec in its long way of international recognition.

This grape produces very pleasant wines, with sweetish floral aromas (especially of roses), yet in the mouth they taste dry. This is one of its most original features. But although the majority of the Torrontés wines are dry, there are also some wines produced with this grape that are naturally sweet (similar to "late harvest" wines).

Torrontés plantation, Bodegas Etchart

It may be necessary to understand the Torrontés before talking about its qualities. When it has been properly vinified, it generates wines that create immense sensations and which are totally different to those one is accustomed to, when drinking other white wines.

The best examples are elaborated in the Province of Salta, especially in the region of Cafayate. There are also excellent examples from the Province of La Rioja especially from the area of Chilecito, where the young denomination of origin "DOC Valles de Famatina Torrontés Riojano" guarantees the quality of the product.

The following wines are recommended: Etchart Cafayate Línea Internacional Torrontés 2000; San Pedro Yacochuya Torrontés 1999; Río Seco Torrontés 1998; Santa Julia Cosecha Tardía Torrontés 2000.

Santa Julia Innovación Torrontés Cosecha Tardía Viñedos y Bodega La Agrícola (Bodega Familia Zuccardi)

Riesling ＊ This grape variety is not significant or well known in Argentina, but the same can not be said of the same variety in the region of Alsace in France or at the Rhine or the Moselle regions in Germany, where the Riesling is supposed to come from. Those regions are its favourite habitat and the wines produced there are really impressive.

The Riesling is one of the noblest grape varieties in the world, but in Argentina, where it is grown in a small scale, this grape has not been duly taken into account for, so far. Excellent natural sweet wines can be produced with this grape variety; especially "late harvest" examples but also magnificent dry wines. This versatility is one of its strong points but on the other hand it is also responsible for the difficulty of raising it, as well as for its not easy vinification.

In Argentina, where it is also called Johannisberg Riesling, for its place of origin, it is grown in cold regions such as the Province of Río Negro or the higher regions of Luján de Cuyo, in the Province of Mendoza. There, it tends to produce soft and fresh wines, with the famous characteristics of the variety but without the harmony found in its brothers from Alsace or the Rhine.

It is difficult to recommend an Argentine Riesling, especially because the plantations of these variety are still very small. Maybe the only Riesling varietal that exists in the Argentine market is the Luigi Bosca Johannisberg Riesling 1999.

Luigi Bosca
Johannisberg Riesling
Bodegas y Viñedos
Leoncio Arizu

Earthenware container,
Museum, La Rural
Bodegas y Viñedos

Gewürztraminer ▪ This grape variety also finds its favourite *terroir* in the regions of Alsace in France and the Rhine and the Moselle Rivers in Germany.

The nose always identifies the characteristic spicy aromas of these wines, which are then confirmed in the mouth. In general, the wines elaborated with this variety are dry, but their versatility, characteristic also of the Riesling grape, facilitates the production of excellent natural sweet wines as well.

It was thought that there would be only a remote possibility that some day a wine with these characteristics, be it dry or sweet, could be made in Argentina. And yet some wineries have started this difficult task. A good example is the Bodega La Rural, with its Rutini wines. La Rural produces a wine with 100% Gewürztraminer grapes, grown in the Alto Valle de Tupungato in the Province of Mendoza; we are referring to the Rutini Traminer 2000. It is an achievement, but the resulting wine is different to the wines coming from Alsace. In the nose, the same floral aromas are felt, but the fruit aromas are not the same. It is very soft but very persistent in the mouth.

When this grape does not come from its homeland, then it is usually called Traminer, probably because it is difficult to pronounce and write the original German name. Yet one has to pay attention not to confuse this grape variety with the Traminer grape variety that comes from Italy and which is supposed to be the father of the Gewürztraminer. Gewürz means spice in German so it is thought that Gewürztraminer is just a spicy variety of the Italian Traminer.

Museum,
Bodega La Rural

Rutini Traminer
Gewürztraminer
La Rural Bodegas y
Viñedos

Chenin Blanc ⚊ The Chenin Blanc grape variety also originates in France, in the Valley of the Loire River. In New World wine countries, new oak barrels are used to mature Chenin Blanc varietal wines. This allows the winemaker to give the resulting wine a bit more personality because, although this grape adapts itself very well to different types of climate and soils, the result is a bit spiritless out of his homeland.

In Argentina these grapes are grown in the region of San Rafael, to the South of the Province of Mendoza. There they find their best habitat. However they are also found all over the country where they are used specially in the production of fine blended wines, in sparkling wines and in natural sweet wines. The Chenin Blanc used to be called with other names in Argentina, and, what is worse, with names of other grape varieties. These mistakes have been put an end to when the INTA made a research on all the grape varieties grown in the country. They determined that there was only a clone of the variety grown in Mendoza called Pinot de la Loire. The Chenin Blanc and its clone Pinot the la Loire produce fresh and stimulating wines that are usually very soft.

Pure varietal wines of this grape are difficult to find in the Argentine market, but among those that exist, one can mention the Jean Rivier Chenin 2001, which, is a sincere and simpe wine and with a very good relation price/quality.

Jean Rivier
Chenin
Bodega Jean Rivier
e Hijos

Chenin grape plantation,
Bodegas Etchart

Ugni Blanc ▪ The Ugni Blanc, with almost 3.200 hectares grown in Argentina, is a generous grape variety in terms of yields. This makes it very interesting because, together with other more brilliant vines, it is used for the production of some good, blended white wines. It is also used for the production of sparkling wines.

The main characteristics of this variety are their marked acidity and a soft fruity aroma.

The resulting wines have a light structure, so it is advisable to drink them young.

Pedro Giménez ▪ This is the grape variety most widely grown in Argentina. It has nothing in common with the Pedro Ximénez grape used in Spain for the production of certain kinds of Sherry.

In order not to confuse it with the original Spanish grape, it is called Pedro Giménez "Cuyano", denotating that the grape is raised in Cuyo. It would have been very difficult to completely change the name used for a grape variety widely grown in nearly 20.000 hectares of the 200.000 that the country devotes to wine grapes.

This grape variety has practically nothing to do with the Spanish Pedro Ximénez yet it is currently used in the production of the imitations of the famous Spanish wine: Sherry (also called Jeréz or Xéres).

Apart from this use, which represents only a small percentage of the total of the wine produced with this variety, the Pedro Gimenez Cuyano is, because of the huge quantity available, the grape which is usually present in the blends of the common white wines of Argentina.

What is the Clone of a Grape Variety?

After the successful cloning of the sheep "Dolly" because the exact copy of the genetic structure of a sheep was achieved, everything seems to be possible.

Harvesters, Viñedos y Bodega La Agrícola (Bodega Familia Zuccardi)

In reference to grape variety cloning, the underlying idea is the same, one should be able to recreate with accuracy, for instance, the Merlot used for the production of the famous Château Pétrus of Bordeaux or the Chardonnay used in the best areas of the Montrachet "appélation", in France.

Diversity is what making everything interesting and exciting. How boring the world would be, if it were full of Dollies and of Chardonnays from Montrachet!

The principle of grape cloning is very simple; one has to make successive plantations of a vine shoot of the wanted variety, discarding the new generations of those that do not reproduce with fidelity the characteristics of the original one. This procedure continuous until the "dissident" vine shoots do not appear any more. After several generations of vine shoots, clonal purity will eventually be obtained.

This system has been fiercely attacked because it is said that clonal purity of a vineyard will produce grapes that generate only very simple wines.

Finca La Anita

The Wine Areas

María Domínguez "Transporting Wine", 2002

In spite of being the fifth largest wine producer in the world, Argentina's wine reality is totally different to the reality in Europe. In a country where a gently sloping plain prevails, the contrast with European wine regions is enormous. One would think that extensive plantation with high yields would be the natural solution for the wine production in Argentina but, in the last years, Argentina has reduced its wine producing areas in a 30% to accompany the tendency throughout the world: it is preferable to produce less wine of good quality than plenty of wine of insufficient quality. This is what the international market is asking for.

In Argentina, contrary to what occurs in Europe, the use of a "denomination of origin" system for the identification of the wine produced in a specific region has only recently been introduced and has been adopted in only some regions of the country.

Some day, maybe, this system which is used almost everywhere in Europe, will prevail in the New World wine producing countries as well, but so far the absence of specific regulations in the wine regions of these countries has contributed to a better flexibility (as regards irrigation, for instance), and this has benefited them. So, what Argentine wineries ussualy do at the moment is to just mention the province in which the wine has been made whenever they want to indicate the producing region. In Argentina grapes are grown especially between the 22° and 42° of southern latitude and almost always along the foot of the Andes. These are the best *terroirs* for its cultivation and development.

Nowadays vines are also being cultivated in the Province of Córdoba and in some *terroirs* in Patagonia.

International experts say of Argentina that it is "in the right side of the Andes". This pun explains the geographical reality of the country: the country is at the "right" of the Andes but at the same time, Argentina is in the correct side for the cultivation of grapes because the wine producing areas are protected by the mountains. This huge massif shelters the vineyards, the cool and moist wind that blows from the Pacific Ocean arrives in Argentina as a warm and dry wind, thus contributing to a better maturation of the grape. On the other hand, the sporadic winds that blow from the East create the perfect climate in a semi deserted area of rigorous but dry winters, and summers and autumns of abundant, but not too much sun. The average rainfall is not over 300-400 mm, so artificial irrigation is necessary. This is done with the thawed water thats flows down the Andes.

In winter, the low temperature in many of these areas contributes to the vegetative rest of the plants but frequent hails in summer can be an authentic headache for the farmers.

Protection nets, Viñedos Norton, Mendoza

Protection nets, Viñedos Norton, Mendoza

1 Salta
2 Tucumán
3 Catamarca
4 La Rioja
5 San Juan
6 Mendoza
7 Río Negro

Lately, in order to avoid this loss, the producers have begun investing in large nets to protect the vines from hail.

The affected regions are the areas in the south of Mendoza, especially San Rafael.

However, in spite of this relative homogeneity of the wine producing regions in Argentina, there are important differences as regards the way in which the vineyards are tended. It is true that these differences are not so marked as they are in the principal wine producing areas in Europe, but they are important enough due to the differences in soil, specific micro-climate and variety of *terroirs*. What vintages are concerned, these are more uniform in Argentina than in all other countries that have traditionally produced wine.

If in Bordeaux (France), for instance, it is normal to see in a ten year period, two good years and eight bad, or not so good ones, in Argentina it is exactly the other way round. However, this does not mean that all vintages are of the same quality. This is not so, there is a difference, but the climatic conditions are much more generous in Argentina than in Europe and that makes it practically very difficult to have really bad vintages. However, in not so good years as for instance 1998, due to the influence of El Niño Current, there were wineries that produced very good wine.

Argentina is also fortunate because of an almost total absence of Phylloxera; an insect that can spoil any vineyard that is vulnerable to it. This insect nourishes itself on the roots of the vines and destroys the plants. This advantage allows the vines to be planted directly in the soil without having to graft them on an "American" root (variety of vine, such as the Vitis lambrusca, that originated in the American continent and is not vulnerable to this insect) and thus favours a more authentic development of the grape variety characteristics. In Europe, where the Phylloxera created havoc in the majority of the vineyards in the XIXth century, this procedure is not possible, except for some naturally Phylloxera resistant soils, as for instance, some sandy soils.

Arnaldo B. Etchart
Vino fino tinto
Bodegas Etchart
Cafayate

Bodegas Michel Torino,
Salta

The North

Salta ⚹ In Salta, in the far North, vines are cultivated in the area of the famous Calchaquí Valleys, the surface of which extends from the west of the Province of Salta to the North of the Province of Catamarca, covering the Northwest of the Province of Tucumán, with a very special concentration in the South of the City of Cafayate.

Espalier vineyard, Bodegas Etchart

The climate is dry, with long summers (which allow a good maturation of the grape) with practically no rainfall so that artificial irrigation is necessary. In some areas hails are common during the summer storms.

Vines have been planted on the hills that are between 1.500 and 2.100 meters high because the high summer temperatures in the lower areas are not suitable for the correct development of the vines. In those areas wich enjoy a cooler microclimate, the grapes can have a refreshing natural acidity generating excellent wines, especially those made of Torrontés or the Cabernet Sauvignon varieties.

DON DAVID

*Don David, Torrontés
Cafayate, Salta
Bodega La Rosa,
Michel Torino*

La Rioja ⚹ This area has appropriate soil for vine cultivation, with a dry and temperate climate and with low rainfall, so that once again, it is necessary to appeal to irrigation. The vines have been planted between 800 and 1.400 meters above sea level.

The best fine wines produced with the Torrontés variety come from a Controlled Denomination of Origin(DOC) "Valles de Famatima - Torrontés Riojano" created in 1995. However, one has to be alert because new wines will appear on the market, especially those produced with other noble grape varieties such as the Chardonnay or the Syrah.

*Vineyard,
Bodegas Etchart*

The Centre

Augusto P.
Cabernet Sauvignon
Augusto Pulenta

Serie Reservada
Finca La Escondida
Cabernet Sauvignon
Finca La Escondida

San Juan ✳ San Juan is the second largest wine producing region in the country as regards the total area of implanted vines. Because of this, wine production is very important. In the past, the production of common wines prevailed, a waste, if the fantastic climatic conditions of this region are taken into account.

San Juan is characterised by being quite dry and hot and watering has to be controlled by means of artificial irrigation.

These conditions allow an excellent maturation of the grape under perfect sanitary conditions, which makes this Province a very interesting area for the production of organic or natural sweet wines.

However, the original condition of the soil is compensated by the enormous reforms that are being carried out in the sector, which can already be proven in some of the wines available in the market, as for instance the wines of Finca La Escondida (Peñaflor) or the red wines of the young Augusto Pulenta winery.

Mendoza ∗ This Province is divided into two well-defined regions separated by a desert. To the north, the basin of the river Mendoza, and to the south the Valley of San Rafael.

The northern area can be subdivided into four sub-regions: the North, the East, the High Area of the Río Mendoza and the Uco Valley.

Vines are planted between 500 and 1200 meters above sea level. The climate is dry, but the rivers carry abundant water, which is used for irrigation. The temperature differences between day and night please the grapes, which can attain a well-balanced maturation. Mendoza is cooler than San Juan and has fewer sunshine days. However in summer and in the beginning of autumn the sky is usually clear letting the sun warm the grapes when they need it.

The big annual temperature range is remarkable, allowing a correct vegetative rest of the vine.

Mendoza is the most important wine region in the country, not only because of the quality of its wine, but because of its production as well: approximately 70% of the wine in Argentina comes from Mendoza.

F. Brambilla (1750-1832) "Puente del Inca (Inca bridge), Mendoza"

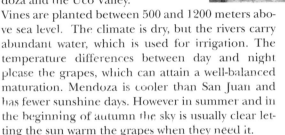

It is important to emphasise the significance of the wines produced in the High Area of the Río Mendoza, especially those produced in the Departments of "Maipú" and "Luján de Cuyo".

Vineyards, Alta Vista Mendoza

Luján de Cuyo DOC is a controlled denomination of origin, which was created in 1989. The denomination of origin Maipú DOC is being organised at the moment.

The region of Tupungato, in the Uco Valley, has exceptionally good conditions and produces some of the best fine wines of the Province of Mendoza, especially white wines.

The area of San Rafael, a gently sloping valley, has an average altitude of 500 m to 800 m. Although it is a region in the South of the Province, the area is protected by the hills called Sierra Pintada (also known as Bloque de San Rafael) against the icy winds that blow from the South. The soil of San Rafael is of very good quality, and as for the climate, it is moderately cold, if we consider the sum of the average temperatures. Rainfall is scanty but the Rivers Diamante and Atuel carry a lot of water from the mountains and perfectly make up for this lack of water. Hail seems to be the only problem, it occurs with more frequency than in any other part of the Province of Mendoza.

Nieto Senetiner, Malbec Bodegas Nieto Senetiner This is the first Malbec with DOC Certificate in South America.

Given the distinctive characteristics of the wines of this area, a denomination of controlled origin was implemented: "San Rafael DOC". The regulating office that created it, is one of the most active ones in the country.

The South

Río Negro ≈ Río Negro, (Black River), is probably the southernmost wine region in the world with its vineyards planted between the parallels 37°30' and 40° 30' southern latitude. This surely has some influence on the distingtive characteristics of the wine from this Province.

Vineyard and Valley of the Río Negro, Establecimiento Humberto Canale

Vines are cultivated in five valleys that run from east to west. In all of them the climate is continental and desert-like, with very low rainfall (195 mm) and where it is necessary to water the vineyards with artificial irrigation. There is a broad temperature range between day and night, which allows the grape to mature correctly. Hails are not an economic problem in Río Negro because they hardly ever happen. The real problem in Río Negro is frost, which shorten the vegetative period of the grapes. This is particularly bad for the grape varieties with long maturation cycle because they cannot develop as they should in this kind of climate.

Canale Black River Reserve Pinot Noir Establecimiento Humberto Canale, Río Negro

Grape varieties with a short maturation cycle such

as the Merlot or the Pinot Noir, on the other hand do not have any problem with these climatic conditions and can take full advantage of the singular soils found in this province.

Wine Production

It is very easy to obtain wine from grape juice. Wine production is very easy in all parts of the world where grapes grow. One can produce wine even at home using traditional methods. If we want to obtain alco-

Crushing and pressing grapes, Bodegas Etchart

holic grape juice, something that might be called "wine", then the only thing we need is to have some recently gathered grapes from the vineyard.

The necessary reactions for the elaboration of wine start spontaneously, if nature is given the necessary conditions.

Which are those reactions?

The most important reaction is alcoholic fermentation, and is nothing but the transformation of sugar into ethyl alcohol.

The yeast that adheres naturally to the skin is responsible for this magic transformation.

In the world there are wineries that resemble space laboratories. They are high-tech wineries, where the

Many cares are necessary to obtain the best wine. However, this was how wine was basically produced since the very beginning.
Things have changed a lot now, obviously.

obsession for perfect sanitary conditions is a constant feature. And where traditional and empirical procedures go together with modern techno-scientific methods. That is what the modern world of wine is like and the wineries have a serious commitment with the client and the sustained quality of all their products.

In Argentina there are some wineries, which are more than a hundred years old and they have an enormous accumulated empirical knowledge. However, their wine used to be of bad quality. This happened in traditional wineries and in younger ones; this happened in big wineries and also in the smaller ones. This happened basically in many wineries. And if they once produced a good wine, then it was probably just by chance.

Press,
Finca Flichman

Today this has changed and the tendency is to restructure the wineries because they have adopted the techno-scientific knowledge as their pattern for success.

Wine production is a science mixed with art. The wine makers have now started talking about different types of vines, of late gatherings, of stainless steal tanks, of temperature control, of a long maceration, of a fermenta-

Bottling plant,
Bodegas López

tion with selected yeast, of new barrels made of oak, of "brut nature" sparkling wines... all this because there is a competitive market, because there are demanding consumers and because the world of wine is so exciting!

Stages in Wine Production

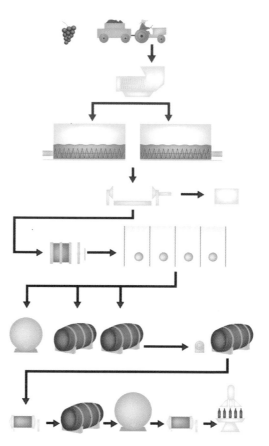

Vintage
Transport

Grape reception
Press

Press
Addition of sulfur
dioxide

Press and separation
of marc

Heater (optional)
Maceration tanks
(grape juice with grape
skins) and fermentation

Fermentation
tanks/casks/barrels
First clarification
Cask or barrels matu-
ration

Second clarification
Stabilization
Filtration (optional)
Bottling

This process is also used for the production of white and rosé wines. For the production of white wines,
the must, macerated without the skins, is poured directly into the fermentation tanks.
For the production of rosé wines, the red grapes are left with the skins during a very short period of time
so that the must will get some colour.

The Production of
Sparkling Wine

Dom Pérignon, a Benedictine monk in the Champagne region in France, is traditionally asumed to hace discovered the procedure used to produce sparkling wines. It happened at the end of the XVIIth century, probably by chance.

Dom Pérignon realised that some of his wines refermented in the containers where they were stored. This refermentation released a gas that combined with the wine, gave it a fizz that the monks of the Benedictine monastery of Hautvilliers liked very much. The second fermentation in thicker bottles that Dom Pérignon ordered to be manufactured and the use of corks made of the bark of the cork oak to guarantee a perfect conservation of the fizzed content, was the monk's invention.

"I'm drinking the stars" said Dom Pérignon as he tasted his champagne

The system used to produce sparkling wine, a wine with gas caused by a second fermentation and not just an addition of gas, is the same all the world over. However there are several methods to produce this type of wine. The most famous methods are called "champenoise" (also called traditional or classical) and "charmat". The big difference between one and the other lies in the container in which this fermentation generates the characteristic gas of champagne (carbon dioxide).

In the "champenoise" method, the second fermentation takes place in the bottle, whereas in the "charmat" method, the second fermentation takes place in big tanks, preferably stainless steel tanks, where the wine is stored.

Malbec Espumante Tinto (Red wine) (Sparkling wine) Champenoise method Viniterra

In general, in order to produce a second fermentation, one has to add sugar and yeast to the original wine.

The exception to this rule occurs in champagnes produced by a method, which some people call "rural method".

In this case, the original wines already contain the necessary residual sugar needed to favour a second fermentation and the formation of carbonic gas as a consequence.

Bodegas Chandon

In the second sugar fermentation, one of the resulting products is the gas CO_2 (carbon dioxide). In the first fermentation, called alcoholic fermentation because it is responsible of the transformation of the grape juice sugar in alcohol, carbon dioxide is also released, but this gas in not made use of and looses itself in the air.

The "champenoise" method is considered the authentic method. During fermentation, the pressure inside the bottle can reach up to 6 atmospheres, much more than you would find in a pumped up tire. This is the reason why the bottles used are thicker than the conventional still wine bottles.

After finishing this second fermentation, something called "dégorgement à la volée" or disgorging takes place. With this procedure the sediment (rejected mineral salts and vegetable matters such as dead yeast and other precipitated compounds) which has accumulated in the neck of the bottle, is taken away. The bottle covered with a special capsule is placed in an almost vertical position with the top pointing downwards to enable the deposit to start sliding down towards the neck. Generally, the liquid in the neck is frozen, so the bottle is opened and the wine in the neck, which contains the sediment, is expelled thanks to the force of the carbon dioxide formed inside the bottle. The bottle is then covered again, but this time with the definitive cork. In order to replace the small amount of lost liquid, the so called "liqueur d'expédition" or dosage is added. It usually consists of stabilised pure sugar cane syrup dissolved in old champagne, wich will give the champagne its definitive personality and will eventually give the sweetness of the final wine. This dosage varies from winery to winery and from different champagnes of the same winery. Each champagne brand has its secret and there are some wineries even that add cognac to their "liqueur d'expédition" formula.

In France, the authorised grape varieties for champagne production are Chardonnay, Pinot Noir and Pinot Meunier. In Argentina all grape varieties can be used, the selection being made by the wine maker. However the most widely used varieties are Chardonnay, Ugni Blanc, Chenin, and more often than not, Pinot Noir. These grape varieties are rarely used on their own; in Argentina, to make sparkling wine, blends of two or more different varieties are used. In France, the champagne produced with Chardonnay grapes is called "Blanc de Blancs" (white of whites), and this denomination will always appear on the label. In exceptional vintages, the wine maker will produce what is called a champagne "millésiné".

Stages for the production of a champagne cork. The characteristic mushroom-form develops when the cork is pushed into the bottle.

This type of champagne is not the result of a blend of various year base wines, but of grapes from one single year harvest. These are generally the most expensive wines, and they usually age well in the bottle. However one should bear in mind that champagne

Bodegas Bianchi

is sold when it is already fit for drinking: it is not a wine that should be stored in a bottle for a long time. Champagne without a vintage date, that is, when it is not "millésimé" has already spent some years in the bottle, so once bought, it should be ready to drink. It should not be stored for more than two or three years.

On the other hand the "millésimé" champagne allows a longer storage, sometimes more than eight years, some even resist fifteen years. They will develop several aromas; they may taste and smell of coffee, chocolate or toast. If the consumer does not like this taste, then it is better to drink it while it is still young. Apart from the traditional champagne, one can also find champagne rosé, the only French rosé wine in which it is allowed to blend red and white wines. This champagne is very exotic and also very expensive. It is quite difficult to produce.

Champagne rosé is one of the most seductive and luscious wines in the world!

Champagne cork just extracted from the bottle with its characteristic mushroom form.

Brut or Demi-Sec?
Which One Should be Chosen?

Champagne is classified according to the quantity of sugar that the "liqueur d'expédition" contains when it is added. So, in France a champagne stated as "brut" has between 0 and 10 grams residual sugar per litre while a champagne "demi-sec" contains 24 to 35 grams residual sugar per litre.

*Chandon
Cuvée Reserve
Bodegas Chandon*

This description varies from country to country and, in Argentina, the national sparkling wines are qualified with the following names: "brut nature", "extra brut", "brut", "seco" (dry), "demi-sec" and "dulce" (sweet). The drier ("brut nature", "extra brut" and "brut") have a proportion of sugar inferior to 1,5%, while the sweeter ("seco", "demi-sec" and "sweet") have more sugar and they can, in the case of the "sweet", have more than 8% of the total content.

Mont Reims

*Montchenot
Espumante Nature
Bodegas López*

In general a champagne is better, if it has a low content of residual sugar. This means that the second fermentation was as complete as possible and that the taste elements of the added "liqueur d'expédition" has in its constitution a higher percentage of old champagne than of sugar cane syrup.

*Montchenot
Espumante Extra Brut
Bodegas López*

The most important brands of champagne in France only produce "brut" or drier categories of champagne (the denominations "brut nature" and "extra brut" are not used in France). In the case that the champagne has 0 grams per litre of residual sugar, then it is called "brut zero" or "brut sauvage". In Argentina the equivalent would be "brut nature", with the only difference that, however dry the sparkling wine might be, it will never be completely free of a certain small percentage of sugar.

*Mont Reims
Espumante Demi Sec
Bodegas López*

"Champagne" in Argentina

Barrels,
Bodegas Chandon

Baron B. Brut Nature
Millésimé
Bodegas Chandon

Montchenot
Brut Nature
Bodegas López

It is necessary to explain that "Champagne" is a French denomination of origin. Only the wines of that region can use the name "champagne."

In Argentina, this name is commonly used on the labels of the bottles of sparkling wines.

However, this constitutes a clear infringement to the European denominations of origin and it has caused a commercial crisis between countries in Europe and the New World wine contries that use them improperly.

When Chandon, the first French company that settled in Argentina, began to manufacture its sparkling wine in 1959, the consumption habits changed and the national "champagne" became a reference of quality.

Today everybody drinks this wine and for the most varied occasions, with an appetiser, with the main course, with the loved ones, or with a birthday cake.

Chandon due to a very aggressive marketing strategy when it arrived in Argentina, might be strongly responsible for this change.

Today there are several French wineries that come from the Champagne region that have settled down in Argentina. No doubt, the wine producing areas in Argentina are excellent for the production of sparkling wines.

Chandon
Extra Brut
Bodegas Chandon

People love sparkling wine in Argentina, and it should not be surprising that international companies such as Piper-Heidsieck, Pommery or Cordon Rouge (Mumm) would, sooner or later, settle down and start a national production of sparkling wines.

Nowadays, national sparkling wines are even exported to other countries, especially to the neighbouring countries or to the partners of the Mercosur.

There are excellent sparkling wine examples produced in Argentina with an excellent price/quality relationship.

The sparkling wine from Viniterra called Omnium is one of those examples. It has an accessible price and it is within the quality of what has to be expected from a good sparkling wine.

Other examples are the classic Chandon "Extra-brut" or, also from Chandon, the Baron B "millésimé".

From the López Winery we have an excellent sparkling wine: Montchenot "Brut Nature" and from Bodegas Navarro Correas, the powerful Navarro Correas "Extra brut".

Terra Reserve
Espumante Extra Brut
Viniterra

Nieto Senetiner
Tête de cuvée
Espumante Extra Brut
Bodegas
Nieto Senetiner

Bianchi, Espumante
Extra brut
Bodegas Valentín
Bianchi

Serving Sparkling Wines

Champagne Saucer

These saucer-bowl glasses are used to serve sweet sparkling wine or champagne because they attenuate the luscious sensation of so much sugar.

"Brut", "extra brut" or "brut nature" champagne or sparkling wine should be served as aperitif because they are dry wines. However, they can also get along with entrées or principal courses, but in this last case, more powerful varieties should be chosen, as for instance, the "millésimé" champagne, or any other national sparkling wine of similar structure.

For the purist, the champagne "brut" is the best partner to caviar, as well as for live oysters. The sweeter examples should be avoided, because it is difficult to present one of an acceptable quality. However, a good "demi-sec" sparkling wine can accompany a soft dessert.

Champagne rosé or rosé sparkling wines are quite versatile. Although they are generally dry, they go very well at the end of a dinner with a dessert of, for example, strawberries or raspberries.

This elegant wine can also be served with a "sorbet" between two courses. The sorbet (especially if it is made of grapefruit), and the rosé champagne combine perfectly in its function to relax the palate and restore our taste capacity.

The bottle of champagne or sparkling wine should be opened exactly the moment in which it is going to be served and, unless you have an exuberant personality, noisy explosions of popping off corks and foamy air shows should be avoided.

Champagne or sparkling wines should be opened in a sigh, delicately, rotating the bottle and not the cork.

Once in the glass, watch the bubbles. The quality of the bubbles is seen in their fineness, size and persistence; the finer they are, the better the champagne will be.

Their reduced size is also a good indication of the time that the champagne has spent in the cellar before being sent to the market. It is the time in the cellar that will tune the champagne resulting in finer and more delicate bubbles.

Cándido López (1840-1902) "Naturaleza Muerta"

Champagne and sparkling wines are served cold, at a temperature that varies between 6° and 10°. The only exception is for "millésimé" Champagne. Because of its strong body, it can be served at a slightly higher temperature, 13° to 14°.

To reach this temperature, it is enough to put the bottle for 20 minutes in an ice bucket with water and abundant ice. Take the bottle out once the champagne has reached the necessary temperature. The other alternative is to put the bottle in the refrigerator and leave it there for around 3 hours. Yet one has to bear in mind that the storage temperature of champagne should not be that low. It is not advisable to leave the bottles indefinitely in the refrigerator. If you want an express cooling, you can put the bottle in the freezer for about 20 to 30 minutes, but one has to be careful, because if the bottle freezes, it will explode. This method should be avoided, because it is not healthy for the quality of the wine.

Champagne Flute

Champagne is served in champagne flutes; if possible these glasses should have the form of a tulip. Before serving champagne it is advisable to cool the glasses because then the precious liquid is not going to overflow.

The Wine Life Cycle

Before beginning with this chapter, it is necessary to make it clear that it is not true that the older a wine is, the better it will be. Each wine is a case. There are some that need to age, so that they may be fully enjoyed, and there are others that are already de-

Barrel room, with controlled humidity, Bodega Terrazas

crepit after one or two years. Wine is a natural organic product and as such it can also die.

All wines have a time, a cycle that can be compared to the life cycle of a living creature and why not, to that of a human being.

Men and wine go from childhood, adolescence and maturity to old age. These states will define the personality of a wine as they define the personality of men as well.

Youth ⁂ A young wine can be docile and cheerful, but it can also be rebellious and aggressive. Each kid has his own personality…

Adolescence ⁂ An adolescent wine can be crossing an identification phase; it is difficult to say what will become of it. There may also be a moment of lack of definition and rebelliousness. This is probably the only moment in the life of a wine when it should not be opened. One has to let him mature. Many things are on the brink of happening.

Maturity ✻ The wine has reached its adulthood. In this phase, it will show all its exuberance, its ripeness. Past this phase, the wine, if it is bad, will not turn into a good one, and if it is good it will not improve its qualities, it will just turn into something different.

Old Age ✻ What if we leave the wine a little longer in our small cellar? The moment has come, when it starts changing from maturity - which can last for a long or short time, depending on the wine- to old age.

What is old age? It is nothing but a period in which a wine can give us all its wisdom, everything that it has acquired throughout its life; it can give us something sublime.

However, not all wines are able to acquire this wisdom; in the same way that there are illuminated old men, excellent masters, there are also inopportune, moody old men, laden with bad habits.

Old age is probably the riskiest state in the life of a wine, because the frontier with death is very close, so much so, that one might fail to differentiate it

Death ✻ Death doesn't always come after old age. There are cases in which a wine, just as a human being, dies before having finished, or even begun, its life.

Wines can die by oxidation, by the action of bacteria, or simply by contamination.

If a wine dies, there is no miracle that will bring him back to life.

Ageing in bottles, Finca Flichman

The Three Main Defects of Wine

Oxidation ▪ The process of oxidation is more common in white wines than in red wines, but any wine can oxidise if it comes into excessive contact with air. An oxidised wine looses its characteristics and it is then usually compared to Sherry because its aroma and its taste resemble that of this naturally oxidized wine.

Carlos Morel (1813-1894) "Singing at a Pulpería (tavern)" (detail)

Acetic Vinegary ▪ Wine has been attacked by acetic bacteria, which transform wine into some kind of vinegar.

"Taste of mould" ▪ Although the blame of this problem has always been put on the cork (hence the expression "corked"), some years ago it was proven that this scent or taste of mould or of wet cardboard, was mainly due to a compound called TCA (trichloroanisol), which can contaminate, not only the cork but also the wood barrels where wine is being stored. To avoid this problem, the winery has to be in perfect sanitary conditions. Although it is not toxic, trichloroanisol is a popwerful contaminating agent, affecting the aroma and the taste of the wine in an irreversible way.

F. E. Vidal (1791-1861) "Wine Mules"

The Storing of Wine

Which are the wines that can be stored?
Which are the wines that should be stored?
Which are the wines that have to be drunk right away?

*Sala de Barricas
Alta Vista*

*In Argentina, the
excellent quality of
some terroirs produces
grapes with a great
quantity of acids and
polyphenolic com-
pounds, so much so
that wines have a big
ageing capacity.*

These questions, although they are appropriate
questions, do not have absolute answers.
There are six factors that will influence the capacity
of evolution and preservation of a wine: acidity, tannin, alcohol, free sulphur dioxide (SO2), environmental conditions and cork.

Acidity ⁑ Not the total but the real acidity (pH) of a
wine will protect it from the attack of certain bacteria, because most of these living organisms will not
be able to live in an acid environment.
This acidity gives the wine the necessary stability
through time. While being stored, the wine looses
acidity because many of its components, combine

and precipitate in the bottle. Moreover, these acid components are important because they will give the wine freshness and colour brightness.

The quantity and quality of acids in the grapes largely depend on the type of soil in which the vine is grown. Nevertheless, whenever the quantity of the natural acids present in the grapes is not enough, it is normal to correct the content of acids in the wine, (within the limits of what the law contemplates).

There is still a lot to learn about wine, especially many things concerning its conservation and evolution capacity, which depend on many factors. It is for instance not known why certain wines develop better than others.

Tannin ∗ Tannin, a substance belonging to the polyphenol family (an antioxidant compound found in the skin and in the seeds of the grape), is one of the most important elements in what concerns wine ageing capacity in the bottle. Tannin leaves an astringent and dry sensation in the mouth. Try to chew the seed of a grape and you will experience a similar sensation, this is due to the high content of tannin in the seeds. As time goes by, tannin is polymerised, and becomes much softer. This is the reason why the sensations of astringency and roughness are less intense in mature or old wines than in younger ones.

Cross Section
1 Seed
2 Epidermis
3 Vessels
4 Pulp

Alcohol ∗ Ethyl alcohol and acids have similar properties as they both can perform as antiseptics; alcohol is also responsible for the harmony of the components of the wine. It helps dilute the colouring matters and gives wine its structure. We can say that without alcohol wine would not have a frame and we would not be able to call wine by its name.

Sulphur Dioxide ∗ This element does not exist naturally in the grape and it is not a product of alcoholic fermentation either, although according to recent studies, it sometimes might result from the fermentation process.

Lengthwise Section
1 Epidermis
2 Pulp
3 Seed

Viniterra

It is a very efficient antiseptic that is generally added to the wine before it starts to ferment because it hinders the development and activity of certain bacteria that are capable of completely spoiling the future wine. When there is too much sulphur dioxide, the wine tastes of recently burnt sulphur (similar to the scent of recently used matches). If the wine smells of rotten eggs, then it is the result of a sub-product of sulphur dioxide, called hydrogen sulphide, the substance used in stink bombs.

These defects are more common in white and rosé wines than in red wines. Nevertheless, today those two faults are only found in wines from wineries definitely not committed to quality.

Environmental Conditions ✳ These conditions are of course not found in the wine itself but are important factors that have to be taken into account because they determine the conditions for proper wine conservation. Light, as well as excessive temperature can work as catalysers of certain bacteria and the result will be its premature spoilage.

Cork ✳ Cork has to fulfil two important functions: prevent the wine from escaping and isolate it, so that it does not come into contact with air.

The absence of oxygen in a bottle or at least the impossiobility of oxigen renewal in its interior, is a necessary condition for the correct evolution of the wine.

This will not only prevent an eventual development of aerobic bacteria (bacteria that need oxygen to live) capable of spoiling the wine, but it will prevent oxidation as well. That is the reason why a cork is so important for the wine.

Finca Flichman

Cork, made of the bark of the cork oak, is a natural blocker and has perfect elasticity. If it is faulty or was incorrectly inserted in the bottle, then it will not fulfil its purpose and it will allow the air to enter the bottle, contributing with the oxidation of the wine with the passing of time. Oxidised wine will loose its most important organoleptic characteristics and its colour, aroma and flavour will be modified.

Bodegas Luigi Bosca

If you identify a wine as having aroma and flavour that remind you of Sherry wine, then the wine is oxidized. Wine bottles should then be stored lying down and the cork should always be in contact with the wine to remain moist and swollen in order not to loose its elastic characteristic. However, if you are going to drink the wine within its first year then the bottle can remain standing up.

There is also a synthetic material used to close wine bottles, and it is said to be as good as a cork.

*Bodegas
Nieto Senetiner*

Nevertheless, an artificial stopper will not expand or contract accompanying the dilation or contraction of the neck of the bottle which can allow the wine to flow out or the air to get into the bottle. This is considered to be one of the main defects of these synthetic closures.

Finca Flichman

Bodegas Chandon

If wine is a natural product, the result of a romantic effort of man and nature, why should it be locked in a bottle with a piece of plastic?

A natural cork can only occasionally transmit an unpleasant mouldy aroma that will ruin the wine but when the cork is of good quality, it is incomparable and the only alternative for serious wines.

A good cork will maintain its characteristics between 25 and 50 years. However, it can accompany and allow the correct development of the wine in a bottle for much more time.

*Bodega
Navarro Correas*

Other Factors that Influence the Storing of Wine ✳ Apart from these factors, there are others that influence the storing of wines. They are more difficult to be defined since they do not always obey the same rules and scientists have not been able to explain them so far. It is known that the ageing potential of a wine does not only depend on the grapes used nor on the technique applied in its production. It is accepted that this potential is closely related to the climate and soil, the *terroir*, where the vine is grown. Wines rich in tannin and other polyphenolic elements have a better developing capacity than the lighter wines, which have less tannin and less colouring matter. Red wines have, in general, a better capacity for being aged than white wines, because when being vinified, they remain in contact with their skin and seeds for a longer time than white wines. Skin and seeds are the parts of the grape with the largest quantity of tannin and other plyphenols. But there are also some white wines that do have the possibility of a long-term developing. Apparently, special soil and climate are responsible for this. The region of Montrachet, in France, is one of those rare places delivering exceptional long lasting whites. There, only the Chardonnay grape variety is grown and the resulting white wines have to remain in the bottle for ten to fifteen years at least, before they are in their best phase.

In Argentina there are certain regions in Mendoza, especially in the higher areas of Tupungato, Agrelo and Perdriel, where excellent white wines are being produced, not only with the Chardonnay grape, but also with other good white varieties, such as the Semillón.

Ageing capacity does not mean ageing quality. As it has already been said there are brilliant old men and there are bad tempered old men.
Certainly, both are alive, but which of the two have completed their mission on earth?

The Cork Oak

Carlos Morel (1813-1894) "Singing at a Pulpería (tavern)" (detail)

The Cork oak (Quercus suber) is a tree that takes from 25 to 40 years to grow to full size. Then it needs 9 additional years to grow the first useful bark (the "skin"). From then on it is necessary to wait for another 9 years for each production. The cork is extracted from the central part of the bark, in only one cylindrical piece. However, there are corks, which are manufactured with the agglomerate of small bark fragments. This type of cork does not have the same excellent properties as the one-piece cork, but it is a good alternative for wines that are not intended to be stored for long periods.

Portugal is the first world producer of corks, with more than 70% of the international market.

Removing the bark of a cork oak

The cork oak tree needs a special soil and climate to grow. Those conditions are mainly found in Portugal and other Mediterranean countries.

Cándido López (1840-1902) "Yatay Battle" (detail)

What Happens in the Bottle While the Wine Ages?

Finca Flichman

The word bouquet is sometimes used as a synonym of the word aroma. However, it should only be used to define the aroma in aged wines and never in young ones, where there are only primary aromas (aroma of the grape) and secondary aromas (fermentation).

In a practically oxygen-tight atmosphere, that is, in a closed bottle, several reactions will take place. Some of them can be scientifically explained, others still belong to the field of mystery.

Among the reactions that have already been explained, the one called esterification is the most common one: acids combine with alcohol and produce esters, which are responsible for many of the agreeable sensations found in the bouquet of old wines bred in bottles.

The better the quality of the wine, the more complex the bouquet will be. And this bouquet will express everything: the characteristics of the type of grape from which it was made (which are less evident the older the wine); the personality of the terrain where the vine grew; the climatic conditions under which it was made and the properties of the wood where the wine spent part of its life. It is like the result of an important orchestra where each musician will contribute with something special.

Because of this, the cellaring of wine, this patient attitude to let it age and evolve peacefully in the bottle, is so interesting for the enophile, the wine enthusiast.

Cellaring is nothing but the hope that materialises whenever a bottle is uncorked and the heart together with the soul are anxious to cherish what will come. The connoisseur hopes for new sensations, hidden pleasures which, one way or another, end in the conversations with those who share the same passion.

Change of Colour

While the wine evolves in the bottle, many of its components, especially the components that give it colour and structure, combine and finish precipitating in the bottle.

This is the reason why wine, during the process of development in the bottle, will loose the intensity of its original colour and start forming a solid deposit.

The glass on the left contains a young wine (bright red colour), the glass on the right shows an aged red wine (there are already hues of brown). Red wines loose colour as time goes by.

This deposit will be larger if filtration and stabilisation before bottling have not been made.

A wine with deposits is not a bad one, because a deposit is the result of a natural development. When the wine has a substantial deposit, decanting is advisable. Before decanting a wine, the bottle has to remain in an upright position between 24 and 48 hours for the loose deposits to settle down on the underside of the bottle, so as to facilitate the procedure.

It is evident that, in the case of white wines, this problem does not exist, since deposits during the development in the bottle are practically non-existent.

Sometimes some crystals may form at the bottom of the bottle but they will never be solid deposits. In the evolution process of white wines, the colour, instead of fading, begins to gain intensity, changing from soft yellow to an intense gold.

The left glass shows a young wine (pale yellow, sometimes even with greenish tints), while that of the right shows an aged white wine (intense golden yellow). In white wines, the older it is the darker is its colour.

Wine and Wood

Before the wine is bottled and sent to market it is usually kept in casks, barrels, tanks or any other container allowed by law. The same six factors, which were already explained in the chapter about conservation and evolution of wine in the bottle, influence the wine while kept in these recipients.

Wood casks,
Bodegas López

The big difference lies in that inside these recipients, the reactions take place in the presence of oxygen and, in the bottle, the changes happen almost without oxygen.

Old barrel label,
1900, Bodegas López

When in these containers, wine gradually comes into contact with air and consequently with oxygen. This quantity of air, in spite of being small, is going to influence the process of evolution inevitably, causing a progressive and slow oxidation. This gradual oxidation will benefit the quality of the wine, especially the "hard" and astringent one.

Oak barrel from
Slovenia,
Bodega Ruggeri

One way or the other, the evolution of wine through time, be it in these containers (evolution mainly through oxidation) or in bottles (evolution mainly through reduction) pursues one and the same aim: give the wine elegance, softness and complexity.

Barrels,
Bodegas Etchart

Oak Barrel Maturation

In Argentina, the use of oak barrels, especially those called Bordeaux barriques (225 litres) is quite recent. It was in the 90s when these barrels began to be used, because traditionally the wine makers preferred large, old casks.

These oak barrels are chiefly used for the maturation of wines, mainly red wines. However, they are also used for alcoholic fermentation of white wines, especially those produced with the Chardonnay grape variety.

Oak barrels, if properly used, are excellent containers for the evolution of wines. Apart from making them softer, barrels allow wines to age more rapidly and give them complexity and interesting aromas, as for example a very characteristic vanilla aroma.

When these aromas are well integrated with the wine, it means that they are evenly blended with the fruit aromas and the alcohol. The result is a model of elegance. But, obviously, not all wines can get this perfect integration with oak wood. There are cases in which the aroma of wood exceeds the fruit aroma and the result is a heavy wine with no harmony at all. As time goes by, the walls of the barrels transfer part of its components to the wine. One of the most important components is tannin, because oak wood is rich in tannin. This helps the wine develop its structure. It is for this reason that it is generally accepted that the wines bred in oak barrels are better prepared for a posterior development in bottles.

Bodegas Nieto Seneti-ner, Merlot
Wine aged in aok barrels.

French oak barrel, Bodega Terrazas

However, if the wine is bad, no oak cask will ever be able to save it: wine starts to be made in the vine and from then on it has to be taken care of, if the result has to be a wine of fine quality.

Oak barrels, Bodega Terrazas

In the counter-labels we sometimes find indications about wine maturation in barrels.. We may find something like "aged in second-use oak barrels". What does this mean? It means that the barrels used are not new and that they have already been used before.

Oak looses some of its main characteristics after its first use. In general, the best wines are bred in new barrels, which are then used again for wines in which the aroma and taste of oak wood is not so important. Sometimes, part of the wine is aged in used barrels and part of it in new ones, or part of the wine is aged in new barrels and part of it is kept in stainless steal tanks. It all depends on what the winemaker wants to obtain. Oak barrels come from different countries and have different characteristics. Nevertheless, the most widely used barrels in Argentina are made out of oak wood from the United States or from France. There are also some barrels made of Russian oak wood or even from oak of other European countries such as Slovenia.

Bodegas Valentín Bianchi, Enzo Bianchi Wine aged in oak barrels

The selection of the characteristics of the barrels (French oak, small grain, etc.) will depend on the wine that is going to be aged in it and it will also depend on the winemaker's choice.

Barrels made of American oak and stainless steel tanks in the background.

The counter-label can also refer to the time that the wine has spent in the barrel. The higher or lower contribution of the characteristics of oak wood will also depend on the time that the wine is in the barrel. The longer it is there, the more oxygen it will get. But the winemaker is not looking for an oxidised wine; he is looking for a softer and a more complex wine. This is the reason why the development in wood has to be closely controlled so that the wine will just get progressive micro- oxygenation (through the pores of the wood) and not an instant and exaggerated oxygenation. To avoid this unwanted deffect, the barrels will have to be always full and the loss through evaporation has to be immediately compensated.

Wines are bred in oak barrels mainly because of these three reasons:

Barrels, Finca Flichman

※ *Improve their structure, especially its tannin levels.*

※ *Add more elements and thus increase the amount of sensations that wine will create.*

※ *Round up the wines, speeding up their evolution and making them softer and less astringent.*

Large Oak Cask Maturation

Large casks, which have a much bigger capacity than barrels, are still used in Argentina.

Casks,
Bodegas López

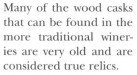

Many of the wood casks that can be found in the more traditional wineries are very old and are considered true relics.

The relationship between the capacity of a large cask and the surface of its walls is much lower than in a barrel. A much lower wall surface will then be in contact with the air. The progressive oxidation will be much slower in these large oak casks.

Vino Fino Tinto López
Aged in French
oak casks.
Bodegas López

Practically no oak wood properties will be transferred to the wine aged in these casks, because they have, in general, been used for quite a long time and the wood has lost most of its principal attributes. However, these casks still have the osmotic property of allowing micro-oxygenation, which is so important for the progressive evolution of the wine.

Although the new Argentine wineries rarely use this kind of containers for the maturation of their wines, there are some more traditional wineries, as for instance Bodegas López, that still use these recipients in the production of most of their red wines. This gives them a very special style.

Chateau Vieux
Aged in French
oak casks.
Bodegas López

The long stay in casks makes the wine loose much of its original colour and when it finally reaches the market, the colour is already brick red. It generally smells of Port wine, yet not as intense as Port wine. They are elegant and soft wines in the palate.

In general, ageing time in casks is complemented with bottle ageing, where some reductive aromas are developed, making the bouquet of these wines even more complex. Nevertheless, there are only a few wineries that can efficiently control the development of this maturation in large casks. Less careful wineries frequently do not compensate the loss through evaporation, which results in a larger surface of the wine coming into contact with the air. This will harm the wine because it starts oxidising abruptly. If we add to this fault, the lack of a good sanitary conservation of the casks, then the only possible result is an oxidised wine, which can have a rancid smell and taste, or it can smell and taste of wet cardboard or even of mould.

Fortunately, this is something related to the past not to the present and future.

One of the last tendencies of well-known Argentine winemakers is to elaborate wine in these large wood casks again. The only difference is that the casks chosen are made of very good oak wood and they are very well taken care of.

The process of maturation in these recipients is strictly controlled: the loss by evaporation has to be immediately compensated. The result of all these efforts is a structured wine, fruity and, if the development time was not exaggerated, with no harmful oxidation.

Cask at the entrance of Bodegas López

Small oak casks, Bodega Norton

Maturation in Stainless Steel or Concrete Tanks

These types of containers are intended to store the wine rather than mature it. They are also used to make the alcoholic fermentation of the wine.

Cement tanks

In stainless steel tanks, the temperature of the fermenting process is controlled through a refrigerating mechanism which allows the winemaker to get a a better controlled extraction of aromas, which was impossible with the methods used before. Besides it is easy to have these tanks in perfect sanitary conditions and no aroma or taste will interfere with the must or wine because stainless steel is totally innocuous. The final result is a fruity wine, where the primary aromas (those belonging exclusively to the grapes) are the most evident ones. These tanks are widely used especially for those wines prepared with an intention of expressing the varietal character of the vine.

In Argentina, concrete tanks were used because they were much cheaper than stainless steel tanks.

The temperature control in these containers not only helps to control fermentation, but to stabilise the wine before bottling as well, because the low temperature will contribute to the precipitation of small crystals that are formed during the process.

The tanks made of concrete are cheaper than the stainless steel tanks. However, they neither have the same sanitary benefits (to compensate this and other isolation drawbacks, the walls are sometimes covered with some type of neutral epoxy resin) nor the same incorporated systems which control the temperature.

Stainless steel tanks, Finca Flichman

Label Interpretation

Bonarda
Bodegas
Nieto Senetiner

Colección Privada
Navarro Correas
Cabernet Merlot
Malbec
Bodegas
Nieto Senetiner

In Argentina, there are still some wineries that do not mention the vintage year on the wine label because they sometimes blend several vintages. This is a matter of style rather than quality of the final product.

Alcoholic Content ∗ Indicates the quantity of pure alcohol that the wine contains. This quantity is expressed in terms of percentage of alcohol by volume which means that if the label of a wine states 13%, then it will have 13 cubic centimetres of alcohol per each 100 cubic centimetres of wine or, 130 cubic centimetres of alcohol in 1000 cubic centimetres of wine (1litre). If we want to express this quantity in weight, then we have to multiply volume by alcohol density. The density of alcohol is 0,7943, which means that 1litre of pure alcohol weighs 0,7943 kg).
A wine with 13% of alcohol will have 103,259 grams alcohol per 1 litre of wine.

Grape variety ∗ If we are talking about a varietal wine, then the label will mention the type of grape that has been used for its production. In Argentina, the law allows that the winemaker can mention the name of the grape, and call a wine "varietal" if the wine has been produced with 80% or more of the same grape.

Region ∗ Indicates the origin of the grapes. In Argentina, as in all other New World wine countries, winemakers have started to give more importance to regions and their own particular characteristics. This has lead to the implementation of some "Denomination of Controlled Origin" (DOC), like the San Rafael DOC in Argentina.

Vintage ∗ Indicates the year in which the grapes that originated the wine were harvested. It is one of the most important informations of the label because the grape quality usually varies from year to year, and consequently, the resulting wine.

Analysis of INV ∗ Is the number of analysis of the National Wine Institute in Argentina, which refers to the consignment of wine used on that bottle; without this number the wine can not be sold.

Grape Variety

Vintage

Region

Alcoholic Content

Capacity

Analysis of INV

Viniterra, Malbec, Casa Vinícola Viniterra

Capacity ∗ Indicates the quantity of wine in the bottle. The most common bottles of wine have a capacity of 750 ml (0,75 litre). There are also "half bottles", which have only 375 ml. Some wineries are now experimenting with a new bottle size, which contains 500 ml (half a litre). This size is probably the ideal size for a dinner of two. Apart from that, one of the purposes of this bottle format is to allow better wines to be sold cheaper, so that more people would have access to them.

In Argentina volume has to be expressed in millilitres (ml), centilitres (cl) or cubic centimetres (cm3).

Big Bottle Sizes

*Apart from the roman-
tic idea associated to
these giant bottles,
wine ages more slowly
and better in these big
bottles.*

Apart from the normal bottle sizes, there are other
bottles, which are much bigger and can contain
from 1,5 to 18 litres. The names of these gigantic
bottles used in the region of Champagne, in France
are also used in Argentina. These names may sometimes vary.

*Different bottle sizes
of Montchenot,
Bodegas López*

*Terrazas, Malbec,
Bodegas Chandon*

Capacity	Names
1,5 litres	*Magnum*
3 litres	*Jeroboam*
4,5 or 5 litres	*Rehoboam*
6 litres	*Methuselah*
9 litres	*Shalmaneser*
12 litres	*Balthazar*
15 litres	*Nebuchadnezzar*
18 litres	*Melchior*

Flavours that can be Distinguished

Human beings cannot distinguish more than 4 types of basic flavours: bitter, acid, salted and sweet. The substances that make up any type of food will always be within one of these families of flavours.

According to recent investigations carried out on the perception of

Epaminondas Chiama (1844-1921) "Fruit"

the basic tastes, scientists have been able to map on the tongue, where the different taste buds can be found. Taste buds are those small cells on the tongue by which flavours in food and drink are recognised.

Acids, in spite of being identifiable in different parts of the mouth, are especially recognised in the upper and lateral parts of the tongue. That is why, wines with a high content of acidity and tannin, as for instance young wines, are felt in that part of the tongue.

The sensation of bitterness in a wine is recognised at the back of the tongue. Very dry wines, those which have just a bit or no residual sugar at all, or those wines that have a lot of tannin, are felt at the back of the mouth.

At both sides of the front part of the tongue, there is a large concentration of taste buds that identify the salted flavour.

Residual sugar (which represents the quantity of sugar, which naturally or intentionally was not transformed in alcohol) is recognised in the front part and at the tip of the tongue.

1 Bitter
2 Acid
3 Salted
4 Sweet
5 Tactile sensitive area

The Glasses

As the taste buds that identify the different types of flavours are placed in different parts of the tongue, glass manufacturers started producing glasses of different shapes according to the personality of the wine. Nowadays, the principal glass ware producers have a complete range of glasses for each different type of wine.

Burgundy glass for acid wines

Glasses and Flavours

The different shapes of the glasses will drive the wine onto the different taste buds. This will help the drinker taste the harmony and balance of all flavours of a wine. For instance, if one is in the presence of a wine of high acidity, it is better to use a Burgundy glass, because this glass will drive the wine straight to all other sensitive sides of the tongue, but the upper part, in order to avoid an excessively direct contact of the wine with the taste buds that will identify this flavour.

In this way, acidity is not tasted directly but all other tastes are. If acidity would prevail, all other tastes would be toned down.

Bordeaux glass used for red wine

The Glass and the Sight

Glasses should be colourless and of the best quality possible. It should be made of sufficiently thin crystal so that it will not cause any visual distortion.

The colour, the clarity and the density of the wine have to be perfectly appreciated.

Glasses and aromas

Apart from the form, glass must have a precise capacity. It has to be big enough to allow a reasonable quantity of wine to be served and shaped so that the bouquet can be properly presented to the nose.

This capacity was not studied in order to fill a larger quantity of wine in only one serving, but to help the identification of wine aromas. A large surface will enhance the bouquet. When wine is served in a glass, aromas start being released in the empty part of the glass, depending on the density of each wine. If the glass does not have the necessary capacity, then the aromas will be very near each other or even mix, so that it is going to be very difficult to identify and separate these aromas. The densest aromas, such as alcohol and those that belong to the family of the woods, stay in the lower part of the glass, between the liquid level and the border of the glass. The fruity aromas go directly to the upper part of the glass, and the "vegetable" sensations place themselves between the two.

The more complex the wine the bigger the glass. That is why bigger glasses are used for red wine. White wines, aged in oak should also be tasted in big glasses. You will be surprised.

Glass for young fruity white wines

Cleaning Crystal Glasses

The best way to clean crystal glasses is with the resulting solution prepared by mixing water (the capacity of the glass), 3 or 4 dessert spoonfuls of vinegar and 1 or 2 of salt. This way, the glass will not only be very clean, but the crystal will also shine. A dishcloth made of pure linen should be used to dry a crystal glass because it does not leave any traces, especially fluff. The decanter can also be washed with this solution, only, since it is bigger, one should add more vinegar and salt.

White wine glass

Corkscrew

Old corkscrew

There are corkscrews in all possible forms and prices, what varies is its efficacy.

A Corkscrew should serve only and exclusively to draw the cork out of an upright bottle. Unless you are an uncontrollable collector, try to look for one that will perform this and only this function.

Do not use corkscrews with "wings", because, in general although one tries to avoid it, they perforate the cork and small pieces of bark will fall in the wine.

However, you should not worry if it happen because these small pieces will not contaminate the wine. But one thing is sure to happen: they will fall in the first glass that you are going to serve. So it is better to pour the wine in a glass and to put it aside before you fill the other glasses.

Vertical corkscrew

Those corkscrews that are said to drive out the cork with gas pressure injected into the bottle are not advisable. They are bombs disguised as corkscrews. There are many cases in which the bottle has exploded even before the cork has given the slightest sign of wanting to leave the place where it is comfortably installed: the neck of the bottle.

Winged corkscrew

Undoubtedly not all corkscrews are black sheep within their family. There are some that are truly brilliant (because they are simple) and they are not even very expensive. There are others a bit more expensive and there are even some which are extremely expensive. These are corkscrew s for the giants among wine drinkers.

Gas corkscrew

With one of these corkscrews one can open several bottles in a few minutes. Everything can be done with a simple movement of the huge handle.

Capsule Cutter

A capsule cutter is a necessary gadget of recent invention. Most corkscrews used to have an incorporated penknife, which was used to cut the seal covering the cork. Today a capsule cutter is used and the seal is cut efficiently and neatly. With or without this cutter, the capsules should be cut around the neck of the bottle to avoid in the moment of serving that the wine should touch the rest of the capsule.

Capsule cutter

Blade corkscrew

One-stroke corkscrew

Two-stroke corkscrew

If your budget is limited, then choose a solid conventional two-stroke model. In general these corkscrews are the best option.

Thermometer

The unit of measurement for temperature is expressed in °C.

The thermometer was not made to measure the fever of the wine, obviously. It was invented to measure the correct temperature that the wine should have the moment of serving. Any variation of this temperature will radically change the aroma and flavour of the wine. Try to drink an oak cask/barrel matured Chardonnay at 8° or 9° instead of 14°. You will realise that the wine has no aromas, the aromas are not released. In your mouth it will taste of common white wine and because of this mistake one could be missing a sublime wine. The correct temperature is an obligatory complement to taste a wine in its complete splendour. And if by chance you are at a restaurant and the waiter brings a bottle of red wine above its recommended temperature, be not ashamed and ask for an ice bucket full of water and ice, and wait until the temperature has come down. Some minutes will be enough.

Red wines have to be served at "room temperature". That is between 16° and 18° which was the "normal" temperature of a house in France some centuries ago, when livestock that lived in the ground floor heated the houses.

* *Old red wines from 16° to 20° (max.).*

* *Young red wines from 14° to 18°.*

* *Oak aged white wines, from 13° to 16°, according to the body and intensity of the wine.*

* *Sparkling wines with body or champagne "millésimé" from 13° to 14°.*

* *Young and light red wines such as "beaujolais" from 10° to 13°.*

* *White or rosé wines, from 8° to 13°.*

* *Sparkling wines or champagne from 6° to 10°.*

* *Natural sweet wines and late harvest from 4° to 7°.*

Epaminondas Chiama (1844-1921) "Still life"

The Drop Stop

If the wine is served directly from the bottle, one of the most complicated tasks is to prevent that rebellious last drop from falling on the white cloth when one is filling a glass.

Once again, a brilliant mind invented a gadget, as simple as it is efficient, and if you use it, not a single drop will ever fall again on the tablecloth.

A drop stop is an object that can be bought at well-furnished wineries. It seems to be very cheap, because it is very simple. And yet it is expensive, but if we come to think the amount of money we spare not sending the cloths to the laundry, then it is worthwhile buying it.

The Decanter

The decanter is a glass or crystal recipient, which is used to separate the wine from those loose deposits that form on the underside of the bottle during the process of development.

However, today it is also believed that the stimulus of fresh oxygen that the wine will get during decanting gives it the possibility of having a chance to breathe. It enables the wine, within a short period of time, reveal qualities that would take it more years to develop in the bottle. Yet not all wines will benefit from the action of pouring it into a decanter.

Which are then the wines that will benefit from this operation? There is no definite answer to this question. Each wine is a case for itself, but it can be said that decanting tends to benefit well-structured young red wines and, consequently, wines with a high content of tannin.

The sudden and massive access to oxygen from the air will soften the astringency that these wines have, and it will also help release dormant aromas.

But, decanting can be extremely harmful for certain wines that have been in a bottle for a long time because decanting can make the wine loose its bouquet. The overexposure of the wine to the air will quickly oxidise it and there will be a loss through volatilisation of the principal aromas acquired in the time the wine spent in the bottle. So, if you are not sure of how the wine is going to behave, especially if the wine is very old and you have only one bottle, do not risk decanting it.

Decanter

It is true that experience is the mother of all teachings, but in this case the wine should only be decanted if there is more than just one bottle of the same wine. Of the young Argentine wines, the general rules

Pulpería (tavern)

state that decanting will benefit the majority of the Cabernet Sauvignon (between 1 and 5 years), especially those with more concentration and structure. The same recommendation can be made for the varieties Syrah or Tempranillo, but the positive difference will only be notorious if the wine is well structured

White wines are seldom considered in this discussion about decanting but this groundless rule should not be followed. Unconsciously, white wines are considered to be of inferior status than red wines but this is not true.

It is accepted that most white wines do not benefit from decanting; the rule is: decant only the rich, well-structured wines. A good Chardonnay or Semillón, matured in oak, can be felt more velvety if it is decanted.

Decanting will even help develop a better homogeneity of the serving temperature, with a better release of aromas, not only for red wines but for white wines as well.

Decantation and Montchenot
The Exception that Proves the Rule

*Montchenot
15 Años (years)
Bodegas López*

Montchenot, one of the most prestigious wines of Bodegas y Viñedos López is a blended wine that spent a long time of its life, ageing in large oak casks and then in bottles. They are wines that have a marked development when they reach the market. Not only because of the oxidation that they gained in the casks, but also because of the reductive process suffered in the bottle. Doubtless, they are wines that have developed a characteristic bouquet after their long breeding. According to the rule, these aromas could be lost in the process of decanting. Yet, decanting is absolutely necessary to harmonise the 15 and 20 year old Montchenot. When the cork is removed, these wines only release their most intense aroma, similar to those of Port wine so characteristic of a wine that has spent a long time in large oak casks. When these wines are decanted half an hour before serving, those stronger aromas will decrease in intensity and will give place to the more elegant and delicate aromas of wise old age.

*Montchenot
20 Años (years)
Bodegas López*

*Frech Oak Casks,
Bodegas López*

The Pliers

Pliers (also known as Port tongues) are a curious object, which resemble more a torture instrument than a gadget related to the world of wine. The pliers are used to open

Pliers

bottles of very old wine with an old, tight-fitting cork, which may be liable to break or crumble and which will never resist the action of a corkscrew.

For this reason, somebody invented a very intelligent methodology to open the bottle in an unconventional way. Literally, the bottleneck will be skilfully

broken. This is done by applying the incandescent pliers (which are previously heated with a gas burner) on the neck of the bottle for about 30 seconds.

Immediately afterwards, a brush that has been dumped in cold water is

passed on the same place. The glass bursts and the neck of the bottle with the cork is removed. The bottle is cleaned with a clean cloth and the wine is ready to be served.

This impressive procedure has to be practised with

empty bottles several times before a really old bottle is opened.

This procedure is not very extended. It is mainly used to open bottles of old vintage Port, which is one of the wines that may age in the bottle for a very long time.

In over 25 year old wine bottles, corks become fragile and lose their properties and cannot stand the devastating action of a corkscrew. They will inevitably fall into small pieces.

The Home Wine Cellar

Winery "La Vieja Damajuana" Santa Fe

We should prefer diversity to quantity. Wine tasters and wine lovers like to taste different wines to experience new sensations.

When somebody enters the endless and exciting world of wine, then a change takes place. A change of money for wine. It is not a cheap passion, because one wants to taste the very best wines.

To store wine in order to drink it later is expensive. However, as time goes by, your wines might increase in value. But to tell you the truth, this is not the normal situation.

The science to buy the correct thing is called… well it has no name so far, but it is a mixture of intuition and experience.

Nobody wants to have bad wines in his cellar and the wines that are worth buying are very expensive.

What should be done, then?

The key lies in a good relationship price/quality (value for money) and in choosing a wine of undeniable quality which has not been discovered by "opinion makers" (restaurateurs, collectors and journalists) so far.

What should never be forgotten is that a certain wine was produced to be drunk in the right moment, because the pleasure lies in drinking it. And this is precisely what has to be taken into consideration when we start buying wines for our cellar.

Here are some pieces of advice of how to start a home wine cellar with Argentine wines:

Sparkling wines:
* *2 or 3 bottles, (brut, extra-brut or brut nature).*
* *1 or 2 bottles of a sparkling wine with harvest date ("millésimé") or a reserve sparkling wine.*
* *1 or 2 bottles of a rosé sparkling wine.*

White or rosé wines:
* 6 bottles of white wine without oak (4 from Mendoza and 2 from Río Negro).
* 4 Torrontés bottles (2 from Salta and 2 from La Rioja)
* 6 bottles of white wine with oak maturation (preferably from Tupungato, Mendoza).
* 2 bottles of dry or fairly dry rosé wine.

Light or medium bodied red wines:
* 10 red wine bottles to be consumed within a year (6 from Mendoza, 2 from San Juan, 2 from Río Negro). Choose fruity varietals such as bonarda, sangiovese, malbec or other varietal wines without oak maturation.

Red wines, well structured and of great concentration:
* 12 red wines to cellar during at least 3 years (at least 8 from Mendoza, from Luján de Cuyo and Maipú). Choose wines produced with one (or some) of these grape varieties: cabernet sauvignon, malbec, tempranillo or syrah. Buy also 2 bottles of Pinot Noir to cellar.

Sweet Natural Wines:
* 2 to 3 bottles of "late gathering" especially from grape varieties such as semillón or torrontés. Try to cellar 2 of them for at least 6 years.

Don't forget that the price of the wine is not always directly proportional to its quality!
Try to buy your wine at the same wine merchant. This will only bring benefits because you not only will get better prices but if you have a problem with the wine you will be immediately assisted. The wine merchant is responsible for the wine he sells.

Where Should you Store your Wine?

Wine should be stored in dark places protected from the effects of extraneous smells (do not store your wine in places that smell of mould or paint), free of

Stored bottles, Finca La Anita

draughts, with moderate humidity (around 70%). And the most important factor, the temperature should be regular. The ideal temperature of a cellar should be 10° to 12°, this temperature should not vary more than 4°. One should not forget that the worst thing for a wine is a sudden change of temperature. Bearing in mind all these factors, one gets to the conclusion that the best place for storing wine is the cellar. Yet there are other places that fulfil the requirement mentioned above, such as underneath the stairs or in a cupboard.

If your house does not have any of these places, then there are closets that satisfy all factors: the temperature is controlled, there are no vibrations and the wine rests in the most perfect dimness. Brands such as Eurocave, Vinocraft, Le Cache, and Vinothèque among others present different models and prices. They can store from 50 to 2500 bottles.

The cellar has to be built in such a way, that all bottles should be stored in a horizontal position. The cork has to be in contact with the wine so as to keep it moist and swollen. It should not loose its elastic properties. A good trick to preserve the labels of the wines that we store is to spray them with lacquer, varnish or a fixative. This prevents humidity from affecting the paper of the label.

Wine storing,
Bodegas López.

Food, Wine and Friends

Guillermo Dohme, "Drinking together", 1978

One of the greatest pleasures of a wine lover is to be able to enjoy wine in the company of people who share the same passion. One of the best ways of doing it is to bring his friends together for lunch or dinner, and start opening the bottles, which he has lovingly stored in his cellar. Each course, its wine.

The order of the wine served has to be carefully thought over, because one has to serve the less intense wines before those which have more personality; the drier wines before the sweeter ones and, to finish, one can add that, if we serve wines of different vintages, then the younger wines have to be served before the older ones.

If the aged wine to be served is substantially inferior in body and structure to the other wines that will be served afterwards, then an exception can be made. If that is the case, in order to avoid a "block" of the palate, one can start with the older wine and the younger wine with better structure and intensity will follow. However, we cannot forget that in this sort of dinners, there is a graduation in the quality of the wines to be served. We cannot, after having served an aged wine of good complexity, serve a younger one, which although it may have a good structure, is inferior in quality.

Obviously, during dinner one of the most important topics of conversation will be the wine. Nevertheless, when one gets to the forth or fifth wine, then surely other interesting topics will come up...

There is one important rule, which in reality summarises all the other ones: one has to serve the weaker wines before the stronger ones. That is why the white wines have to be served before the red wines. However there are cases in which the white wines are stronger and more intense than the red ones, then and only then one can serve the white wine after the red one. The only thing that should be avoided is to serve two different wines, white and red, at the same time and during the same course.

When the desserts arrive, then a new phase begins. One has to uncork one or two sweeter wines, depending on the dessert served. In Argentina, the natural sweet wines or the wines elaborated with late harvested grapes may enter the scene. These wines can also accompany cheese.

To finish in glory and to relieve the tired taste buds, one can serve, breaking all the rules mentioned in this chapter, a "brut" or "extra-brut" champagne or sparkling wine. It is very pleasant. Try it!

The great thing about these dinner parties is that one can serve various glasses of wine (not more than two different wines for each course), and offer the guests a well-organised delight. During dinner, the most important topic of conversation is wine, obviously.

However, when one gets to the forth or fifth wine one has surely developed other interesting topics as well...

Eduardo Ungar
"Grand finale", 1994

Food and Argentine Wines

The rules that govern the selection of wines to accompany certain food are difficult to state, only experience and intuition will help in this difficult task. However, a conventional guide has been added, to help the selection of Argentine wines.

Aperitif
* Sparkling wines "brut" or "extra brut"
* Dry rosé wines
* Dry white wines

Entrées or Shellfish
* Sparkling wines "brut" or "extra brut"
* White wines with no oak, dry or with very little residual sugar (not more than 7 to 8 grams per litre) or a fruity wine
* Dry or half dry rosé wine

Salads
* Dry or half dry rosé wine

Empanadas
* Natural sweet white wine, certain "late harvest"

Pasta
* Red or white fruity wines; a well structured wine if the pasta is served with an overwhelming sauce

Cándido López (1840-1902) "Still life" (detail)

Light fish with a delicate sauce or boiled fish
* *Light white wine with no oak*
* *Young red, with delicate fruit and light body*

Valentín Thibon de Libian (1889-1931) "Mademoiselle Papillon"

Fish with prominent taste, salmon, trout or with strong sauce
* *White, lively and with oak maturation, served at the correct temperature!*
* *Strong and medium bodied red wines*
Meat, with or without sauce
* *Strong, persistent, intense red wine*
Desserts
* *Natural or "late harvest" sweet white wine*
Fruit desserts
* *Rosé sparkling wine, especially for desserts with red fruits such as mulberries, strawberries, raspberries or blackcurrants*
Blue cheese such as roquefort or camembert or any other cheese of intense flavour
* *Natural or "late harvest" sweet white wine*
* *Well-structured white wine aged in oak*
Mild cheese
* *White wine such as chardonnay or semillón, aged in oak*
* *Elegant and well structured red wines (they will depend on the intensity of the taste of the cheese)*

The Four Phases of Wine Tasting

To enjoy all the properties of a wine correctly, we have to use almost all our senses.

First we have to analyse its aspect, its colour.

If we slant the glass having a white surface at the back, we will see that the wine forms a sort of tongue around the border of the glass. The colour is darker in the centre of the tongue than around the border. But the colour that really interests us is the colour at the tip of the tongue. As we have seen before, in the case of those red wines, that have undergone a long time ageing, the colour at the tip of the tongue is lighter. White wines behave differently. The colour at the tip of the tongue is darker if the white wine is old. If the white wines belong to the same vintage, then the colour will be more intense if the wine has been stored and aged in oak.

The second step of wine tasting is the most important one and it is in connection with the sense of smell. With a simple inhalation we can perceive a lot of sensations, especially because in some cases the smell may be a warning not to taste the wine at all. Wine is a natural product, any abnormal smell may be the indicator that there might be a problem with it. The nose can reveal all sorts of things, good or bad and it is there that part of the pleasure of drinking wine starts. When drinking wine, we taste when the wine is taken into the mouth but many of the sensations are volatile aromas that we sense in those passages that we have at the back of our throat and which take the air to the nose.

For a correct appreciation, one should make a gentle and long inhalation to get to all layers of aromas.

To smell the bouquet of a wine, the glass should be swilled round so the scents can be inhaled as they ascend. However, the first in-halation should be made with-out rotating the glass because the defects of the wine, are more difficult to detect if they are blended with all other scents.

The identification of aromas is subjective, some people may smell grapefruit while others are pretty sure that it is not grapefruit but pineapple and it may be difficult to say who is right.

Tears that slide down the sides of the glass are nothing but the result of a combina-tion of sugar and alco-hol. The more tears a wine has the higher will be the content of alcohol or sugar, or of both. Tears become obvious when the wine has more than 12% alcohol.

The fact is that both have identified a certain scent, and each has felt it according to his particular sense. That particular aroma has to be memorised and associated to the wine that is being tasted so that the next time it is perceived, one can recognise what sort of wine one is tasting and what sort of grape was used to produce it.

The third step in wine tasting is the appreciation of flavours and textures of the wine.

When the wine is in our mouth, we have to open it a bit and inhale so that some air can pass through the wine. This will help us improve our capacity of iden-tification of aromas in a 30% to 40 % and it will also increase the persistence of flavour of the wine in our mouth

To sharpen the sens-es, one should not smoke while tasting wine, and one should not smoke an hour before drinking. Perfumes should not be used on that day either, in order not to mix aromas.

Once the aspect, aroma and taste have been ana-lysed, one can pass on to the forth step of wine tast-ing. Not all people feel the same when they taste wine. This last phase is like a summary where har-mony, balance and structure are analysed. What was the wine like in the mouth?

Was it persistent?

Aromas of the Main Varietals

Nieto Senetiner Malbec, Bodegas Nieto Senetiner
The label refers to a-romas of red fruit in the wine. It also has plum and vanilla aromas.

Cabernet Sauvignon ✷ The wine produced with this grape variety, smells of green peppers. Aged Cabernet Sauvignon can also have other aromas such as smoke, toast, cinnamon or fruit jam.

Malbec ✷ The Malbec is a strong, fleshy wine that has intense aromas of ripe fruit specially mulberries and plums. In the more matured wines pruduced with this grape variety, more complex aromas appear. They may also smell of vanilla aroma.

Syrah ✷ The Syrah in Argentina does not have the smell of spices as it does in other parts of the world. Here it smells of ripe fruit with something of truffles and mushrooms and sometimes also leather and meat.

Merlot ✷ Aromas connected with the wine made with this variety are doubtless aromas of cherries and ripe plums together with the scent of preserves and candied fruits.

Santa Julia Tempranillo Oak Aged Viñedos y Bodega La Agrícola (Bodega Familia Zuccardi)
Intense aromas of ripe fruit, with a tinge of vanilla, coffee and chocolate.

Pinot Noir ✷ The Pinot Noir smells of soil, mushrooms, truffles, cherries and in the best wines, of tobacco, smoke and sometimes also spices.

Chardonnay ✷ Pineapple, honey, green apple are the typical aromas of the wines made with this grape variety. When they are fermented and aged in oak, they smell of vanilla and milk by-products such as butter.

Sauvignon Blanc ❋ The Argentine Sauvignon Blanc usually smells of grapefruits, peaches, new-mown grass, green apples, pineapples and some of them, also smell of toast.

Torrontés ❋ This wine has easily identifiable aromas because it has an intense smell of flowers, especially roses.

Ernesto de la Cárcova(1866-1927) "Still life" (detail)

Glossary

Acidity: *group of different organic acids found in the must or in the wine. They can be fixed or volatile.*

Aftertaste: *Aromas and sensations left in the mouth after tasting a wine.*

Alcoholic: *wine in which one can feel the alcohol it contains, without being aggressive.*

Alcoholic fermentation: *process of wine production in which the sugar of the grapes is transformed into alcohol, carbon dioxide, and other substances, activated by yeast*

Alcoholic strength: *quantity of alcohol per litre, for instance: 13° of alcohol means that the wine has 130 cubic centimetres of alcohol per 1000 cubic centimetres of wine.*

Ampelography: *science that studies the description of grape varieties and the ways of cultivating them.*

Animal: *it defines the scents connected with meat or leather. Scent found in wines that have been left in old or dirty barrels. It can also be present in wines that have been kept in bottles for a long time. It is usually unpleasant.*

Aroma: *Group of sensations caused by the wine in the sense of smell. They can come from grapes (primary), they can be generated during fermentation (secondary) or develop during ageing (third).*

1 Capsule
2 Neck label
3 Label
4 Counterlabel
5 Punt

Astringent: *wine that leaves a sensation of roughness or dryness in the mouth, tongue and palate because of too much tannin.*

Balanced: *wine with all sensitive qualities playing well together and thus giving pleasure to the taster.*

Barrel: *wood recipient used to store and mature wine. Normal dimensions vary from 225 lts to 300 lts.*

Beefy: *fleshy, thick, strong, dense wine that gives the impression that one can chew it.*

Big: *broad, complete wine, well structured, full of shades. It defines a wealth of flavours that fill the mouth. Possibly, strongly alcoholic.*

Blind tasting: *test in which the bottles are covered so that the taster can draw his conclusions without being influenced by the brand of the wine.*

Body: *term used to refer to structure, consistency and weight of a wine in the mouth.*

Bouquet: *word of French origin that designates all the smell sensations only present in aged wine.*

Brick: *Typical colour of old red wines.*

Brilliant: *luminous and clean looking wine.*

Brut: *a term used to describe natural Champagne or sparkling wines that have very low residual sugar, or no sugar at all.*

Butter: *aroma and flavour that derive from the fermentation carried out in casks of new oak.*

Capsule: *film that wraps the neck of a bottle of wine and hides the cork. It may be made of lead (old ones), tin or plastic.*

Cask: *wooden recipient used for storing and maturing wine.*

1

2

3

4

5

1 Narrow border to preserve the aroma of the wine.
2 Transparent and colourless glass to see the colour of the wine.
3 Curved shape that allows swilling around the wine.
4 Stem to hold the glass without changing the temperature of the wine.
5 Base

Clear: *wine, without visual defects such as particles in suspension. Wine with a good degree of transparency.*

Cloudy: *wine with low transparency.*

Complex: *wine with numerous and well-balanced aromas and flavours.*

Crisp: *cheerfull, lively, bright wine with clean aroma and balanced acidity.*

Damajuana: *carafe, big, basket-like bottle of 4,5 to 5 litres used for standard quality table wines.*

Dark fruits: *term used to refer to aromas and flavours of wild dark red fruits such as berries, mulberries, gooseberries, plums and cherries.*

Decayed: *wine that has lost its initial vigour and quality.*

Delicate: *fine wine but without intense scents and flavours.*

Vat

Dirty: *badly made wine with strange and unclean aromas.*

DOC: *Acronym used for "Controlled Denomination of Origin" and refers to a defined region where wine production is strictly controlled and regulated. The existent DOCs in Argentina ("Valles de Famatina"; "San Rafael" and "Luján de Cuyo") are controlled by a board made up of a group of wineries which founded the DOC region. The wine that carries the label "Denominación de Origen Controlada" has to be produced with grapes harvested in that region and coming from authorised vines. Apart from other legal requirements, a DOC wine has to be accepted by a committee of tasters.*

Damajuana

Earthy: *wine with aromas of recently moistened earth, dry fungi and dust. Very characteristic of Pinot Noir varietal wines.*

Easy: *soft and simple wine, very easy to drink, without edges.*

Elegant: *classy wine with a good balance of colour, bouquet and taste.*

Filtration: *cleaning of the wine from impurities in suspension before bottling.*

Barrel

Fixed Acidity: *group of natural acids found in the grape (tartaric, malic and citric acids) or those formed in the malolactic fermentation (lactic acid).*

Fizzy wine: *foamy wine to which carbonic gas has been added. Usually of bad quality.*

Flat: *wine lacking acidity. Short in sensations.*

Cask

Floral: *scent of flowers (jasmine, rose, violet), common in aromatic white wines such as the Torrontés.*

Fortified: *wine to which brandy has been added, thus stopping fermentation and preventing the total transformation of sugar into alcohol. Wines with a high alcohol content*

Fresh: *wine with balanced acidity and alcohol content.*

Fruity: *wine with strong aroma of the grape varieties with which the wine has been produced or of other fruits. Characteristic generally found in young wines.*

Generous: *big, mouth filling wine.*

Glycerine: *third component of wine apart from water and ethyl alcohol; important element in the structure, flavour and softness of wines.*

Harmonic: *perfectly balanced, edge-less wine.*

Hectare: *a measure of area in the metric system equal to 10.000 square metres (approximately two soccer stadiums).*

Herbaceous: *wine with vegetable aroma and flavour. Sometimes, it means that the grapes were harvested too soon and have not ripened properly.*

Honey: *characteristic aroma of certain fine and mature wines; especially those aged in bottles.*

Husk: *skin that wraps the pulp of the grape.*

Hydrogen sulfide: *chemical compound that has a characteristic scent of "rotten eggs." It is the result of a chemical reaction of the sulphur dioxide in an oxygen free ambiance, like an air tight closed bottle.*

I.N.V. Instituto Nacional de Vitivinicultura: *Board belonging to the Secretary of Agriculture of the Argentine Ministry of Economy created by a national law in 1959. Their headquarters are in the city of Mendoza and it has delegations in the main wine producing centres of the country. Its main job is the technical control of wine production, its industry and trade and the elaboration of statistics. Today it is actively assisting wine makers with wine exports.*

Iodine: *a very special smell and taste usually found in wines that have aged in bottles for a ong time.*

Stainless steel press

Lactic acid: *product of the malolactic fermentation.*

Late harvest: *grapes are picked when they are past the point of maturity. They usually have a larger concentration of sugar. Type of wine elaborated with these grapes.*

Light: *fast wine, with little consistency, generally due to a low content of alcohol and dry extract.*

Maceration: *procedure by which must is put into contact with grape skins in order to obtain colour and aroma. It is mainly used in the production of red wines to obtain deep colour and concentration*

Magnum: *bottle with a capacity of 1,5 litres. Big bottles allow a slow evolution of the wine.*

Malic acid: *natural component of wine, which is turned into lactic acid during the malolactic fermentation. A characteristic aroma of green apples identifies the presence of this acid.*

Malolactic fermentation: *transformation of malic acid into lactic acid, activated by lactic bacteria. It is an almost indispensable process in fine red wines.*

Marc: *skin, and other solid residues of non-fermented grape. A brandy can be obtained by distilling grape residue*

Maturation: *ageing, process of ageing wines.*

Milky: *secondary or terciary aroma in good quality wines similar to the delicate aromas of milk products such as butter.*

Mould: *microscopic fungi that may develop on grapes or in containers where wine is stored.*

Must: *grape juice.*

Noble rot: *whenever attacked by a fungus known as Botrytis cinerea grapes become dehydrated thus increasing their sugar concentration. This rot is necessary to produce the famous Sauterne wines in France and also other natural, sweet wines around the world.*

Oaky: *vanilla like aroma and flavour resulting from ageing wine in oak casks or barrels.*

The Wine Barrel
1 The tap (spigot, vent) hole
2 The bung
3 The bung hole (faucet hole)
4 The cask body
5 The hoop
6 Stave (one of the curved pieces of wood)

Oenology: *science thast studies all the processes of transforming grapes into wine.*

Oenologist: *viticulturist, winemaker; wine expert, person devoted to the wine production.*

Oily: *greasy, wine rich in alcohol and glycerine and sometimes, lactic acid.*

O.I.V: *International Office of the Vineyard and Wine: scientific and technical organisation created in November 29, 1924. Spain, France, Greece, Hungary, Italy, Luxembourg, Portugal and Tunisia were the countries that founded this organisation, which deals with everything connected with wine production and consumption. Today 45 countries have become members of the OIV and Argentina is one them. The OIV represents the majority of the countries that produce wine in the world: 85% of the vineyards in the world, 95% of the world production and 95% of the world consumers of wine.*

Phylloxera

Organic wine: *wine which has been produced with a minimum use of chemical products. They are usually difficult to preserve and age.*

Oxidation: *chemical reaction of the different components of wine which takes place when wine comes into contact with oxygen. It is a necessary process when ageing certain wines, but it can originate serious alterations in them when caused involuntarily. These oxidised wines usually smell and taste like Sherry wine.*

Phylloxera

Persistent: *wine that remains in the mouth after swallowing it.*

P.H.: *Hydrogen Potential: scale (from 1 to 14), that measures the acid or alkali level of a solution or a substance. A reading of below 7 indicates that the solution is acid and above 7 that it is alkaline. Wine acidity is measured in pH.*

Phylloxera vastatrix: *insect that nourishes itself on the roots of the vines and kills the "vinifera" types of vines.*

It created havoc in the majority of European vineyards in the XIXth century.

American vines had acquired immunity by developing the ability to heal the wounds. So Vitis vinifera types of vines were grafted onto American rootstocks to avoid spoilage and death.

American vines, such as the Vitis lambrusca, when not grafted with a Vitis vinifera type of vine, cannot produce grapes fit for the production of wines.

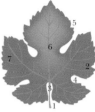

1 The leaf stalk (petiole)
2 Limb
3 Stalk cavity
4 Lateral cavity
5 Serrate leaf margin
6 Midrib
7 Lobe

Polyphenols: *family of organic substances, such as tannin for example, found in the skin and seed of the grape grain. They are of great importance in the final quality of the wine, as well as for its conservation capacity and evolution.*

Press: *container where the recently collected grapes are pressed to obtain must.*

Primeur: *French term applied to the commercialisation of young wines before they go out to the market.*

Reduction: *chemical reaction opposed to oxidation that happens in the absence of oxygen.*

Refresh: *to mix some young wine with old wine in order to give it freshness.*

Reserve: *term used to qualify wines with some sort of ageing. Each country has its own legislation to name a wine "reserve" but in general they are fine wines with a long time of ageing before reaching stores shelves.*

Ripening process: *biological process in which the acid substances in the grape are transformed into sugar.*

Rosé: *pink colour wine produced of red grapes with a very small skin maceration time. The skin is left in contact with the must only for a couple of hours, so that the wine just gets a slight coloration.*

Rough: *wines with too much tannin. They are hard and astringent.*

Round: *wine with harmonic properties, none of them stands out in particular. Wine without edges, but with volume and with plenty of body.*

Short: *wine with short persistency in the mouth.*

Silky: *velvety, soft wine that caresses the mouth, pleasant to the palate.*

Sommelier: *French word used to name the person in charge of the purchase, cellar management and service in a restaurant.*

Sparkling: *wine with natural carbonic gas obtained through a second fermentation of the wine in the bottle (or tank) with the addition of yeast.*

Male leaf of a vitis vinifera silvestris

Structure: *frame of the wine. Combination of the fundamental components: acidity, alcohol, tannin, fruit and sugar.*

Sulfurous dioxide: *chemical compound of sulfur and oxygen that has an antiseptic and antioxidant action in wine. When there is an excess of this element the wine will smell and taste of burnt matches.*

Female leaf of a vitis vinifera silvestris

Tannin: *Organic substance, of astringent action, that is present in grapes (mainly in the skin and seeds) or in the wood in which wine is stored. There is more tannin in red wines than in white wines.*

Tartaric acid: *Main acid found in wine. Wines with little acidity need tartaric acid to improve the quality of the wine and its conservation.*

Terroir: *French word to define an area with characteristic soil and climate that give personality to the wines produced there.*

Tobacco:*some aged wines develop a tobacco aroma.*

Total acidity: *all acids contained in a wine or must; it is generally expressed in grams of tartaric acid per litre.*

Vanilla: *aroma and taste in wines that have aged in oak casks.*

Varietal: *wine produced of only one type of grape variety. Also called monovarietal.*

Varnish: *scent of lacquered wood, of resin, characteristic of very old wines.*

Vertical tasting: *tasting of wines that have one characteristic in common, such as wines of the same winery but of different vintages.*

Flowering periods of the vine

Vinegary: *wine with too much volatile acidity which makes it unfit for consumption.*

Vineshoot: *branch of the vine.*

Vinification: *the process to transform grapes into wine.*

Vintage: *year in which the grapes have been harvested.*

Vitis vinifera: *the only kind of vine, the grapes of which are appropriate for the production of wine.*

Volatile acidity (VA): *group of volatile acids formed during fermentation or as a consequence of microbial alterations; its value is an indicator of wine degradation. Normal in certain quantities, it can be harmful in high quantities. The most important volatile acid is acetic acid, which is an indicator of the transformation of wine into vinegar.*

Yeast: *micro-organisms that start fermentation and transform the sugar of the grapes into alcohol.*

Zonda: *warm and dry wind of the Mendoza region. It usually lasts for over twelve hours. During this tme , the relative humidity of the air decreases enormously, reaching values of 10% to 20%.*

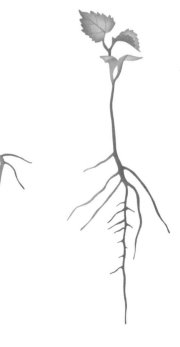

Index